# Tower Vortx Dual Basket Air Fryer Cookbook:

## Healthy & Easy Tower Duo Basket Air Fryer Recipes.

*By Oliver Evans*

# Table Of Contents

Table Of Contents .................................................................................3

Introduction................................................................................. 8

Advantages of Using a Dual Basket Air Fryer ................................................. 10

Understanding the Tower Dual Basket Air Fryer: .......................................... 13

Easy and Iconic Cooking................................................................. 13

Maintaining Your Tower Dual Basket Air Fryer:............................................ 15

A Breeze of a Task ........................................................................ 15

Breakfast Recipes.......................................................................... 18

Crispy Bacon and Hash Brown with Eggs .............................................. 19

Grilled Tomatoes and Crispy Mushrooms ............................................. 19

Apple Muffins .............................................................................20

Banana Walnut Muffins ................................................................20

Veggie-Filled Frittata with Sweet Potato Hash Browns ............................... 21

Zucchini Bread............................................................................ 21

Banana Bread............................................................................. 22

Salmon & Broccoli Quiche.............................................................. 22

Green Veggies Frittata................................................................... 23

Cheese & Cream Omelet ............................................................... 23

Lunch Recipes .............................................................................24

Baked Cod with Roasted Vegetables .................................................. 25

Beef Taco Rolls .......................................................................... 25

Beef and Vegetable Skewers ........................................................... 26

Quinoa and Vegetable Stuffed Bell Peppers........................................... 26

Grilled Cheese and Tomato Sandwich ................................................. 27

Sweet Potato and Chickpea Curry ..................................................... 27

Tofu and Vegetable Stir-Fry ............................................................28

Spinach and Mushroom Stuffed Chicken Breast......................................28

Beef Cheeseburgers .................................................................................................... 29

Salmon and Asparagus Parcels .................................................................................. 29

## Appetizers and Side Dishes ........................................................... 30

Crispy Vegetable Spring Rolls ..................................................................................... 31

Garlic Parmesan Zucchini Fries ................................................................................. 31

Spinach Stuffed Mushrooms ....................................................................................... 32

Sweet Potato and Carrot Fritters............................................................................... 32

Balsamic Roasted Brussels Sprouts .......................................................................... 33

Crispy Kale Chips.......................................................................................................... 33

Mozzarella-Stuffed Portobello Mushrooms ............................................................ 34

Crispy Buffalo Cauliflower Bites ............................................................................... 34

Spiced Roasted Butternut Squash .............................................................................. 35

Crispy Garlic Parmesan Green Beans ....................................................................... 35

## Fish and Seafood Recipes .............................................................. 36

Grilled Lemon Herb Sea Bass..................................................................................... 37

Crispy Garlic Prawns with Roasted Vegetables ...................................................... 37

Tandoori-Style Salmon Tikka..................................................................................... 38

Garlic Butter Shrimp and Herb-Roasted Asparagus ............................................. 38

Lemon-Dill Cod with Crispy Potato Wedges .......................................................... 39

Spicy Cajun Grilled Prawns with Avocado Salad ................................................... 39

Baked Haddock with Mediterranean Quinoa Salad ............................................... 40

Cajun-Style Catfish with Roasted Corn and Peppers............................................. 40

Salmon with Green Beans & Tomatoes ..................................................................... 41

Teriyaki Glazed Halibut with Sesame Broccoli ....................................................... 41

## Poultry Recipes ............................................................................. 42

Balsamic Glazed Chicken Breasts with Roasted Vegetables.................................. 43

Herb-Crusted Turkey Cutlets with Mashed Potatoes ............................................ 43

Lemon-Herb Cornish Hens with Roasted Brussels Sprouts ................................. 44

Crispy Skin Quail with Honey-Glazed Carrots..................................................................44

Spiced Chicken Drumsticks with Sweet Potato Wedges..................................................45

Rosemary Roasted Turkey Thighs with Cranberry Sauce...............................................45

Spiced Turkey Meatballs with Mediterranean Quinoa Salad........................................46

Spicy Buffalo Chicken Wings with Blue Cheese Dip.......................................................46

Mango Salsa Chicken Breast.............................................................................................47

Soy-Ginger Glazed Chicken Thighs..................................................................................47

Buffalo Chicken Tenders...................................................................................................48

Lemon Garlic Roasted Duck Legs.....................................................................................48

Turkey and Cranberry Stuffed Peppers..........................................................................49

Spicy Peri-Peri Chicken Thighs with Coconut Rice.......................................................49

Turkey Meatballs with Zucchini Noodles.......................................................................50

Lemon Pepper Chicken with Mediterranean Rice.........................................................50

Chicken and Leek Pie with Creamy Mashed Potato.......................................................51

Spicy Szechuan Duck with Vegetable Fried Rice............................................................51

Chicken Thighs with Carrots............................................................................................52

Sweet & Spicy Chicken Drumsticks with Potato Wedges..............................................52

**Meat Recipes**..................................................................................................................**53**

Lamb Koftas with Flatbread.............................................................................................54

Lamb Chops with Vegetables...........................................................................................54

Greek-Style Lamb Souvlaki Skewers...............................................................................55

Lamb and Chickpea Stew.................................................................................................55

Lamb and Spinach Curry..................................................................................................56

Lemon Herb Marinated Lamb Steaks.............................................................................56

Lamb Steak and Broccoli Bake........................................................................................57

Rack of Lamb with Green Beans......................................................................................57

Lamb Meatballs and Rice.................................................................................................58

Beef and Mushroom Pie...................................................................................................58

Beef and Bean Chili ................................................................................................ 59

Beef and Pepper Stir-Fry with Rice ......................................................................... 59

Beef and Beetroot Salad with Horseradish Dressing ................................................ 60

Beef Steak with Asparagus ...................................................................................... 60

Pork and Leek Casserole ......................................................................................... 61

Pork Stuffed Cabbage Rolls .................................................................................... 61

Pork and Pineapple Skewers ................................................................................... 62

Pork Chops with Tomato & Onion .......................................................................... 62

Pork with Bell Peppers ............................................................................................ 63

BBQ Pork Chops ..................................................................................................... 63

**Vegetable Recipes** ................................................................................... **64**

Air-Fried Green Beans ............................................................................................. 65

Roasted Brussels Sprouts ......................................................................................... 65

Crispy Carrot Chips ................................................................................................ 66

Air-Fried Asparagus ................................................................................................ 66

Zucchini Fritters ..................................................................................................... 67

Parmesan Roasted Cauliflower ................................................................................ 67

Butternut Squash Fries ............................................................................................ 68

Garlic Roasted Mushrooms ..................................................................................... 68

Sweet Potato Wedges .............................................................................................. 69

Curried Eggplant Slices .......................................................................................... 69

**Desserts** ................................................................................................ **70**

Apple Crisp ............................................................................................................. 71

Baked Bananas ........................................................................................................ 71

Air-Fried Scones ..................................................................................................... 72

Oatmeal Cookies ..................................................................................................... 72

Fruit Skewers .......................................................................................................... 73

Baked Plums ........................................................................................................... 73

Air-Fried Rice Pudding.................................................................................74

Poached Pears in Red Wine.........................................................................74

Brownie Muffins .........................................................................................75

Berry Crumble .............................................................................................75

**Conclusion** ...........................................................................................**76**

# Introduction

Are you among those captivated by the air fryer craze, marveling at its incredible contributions to healthier eating? These nifty kitchen gadgets have become the ultimate game-changer, helping us create scrumptious, crispy delights while contributing to our fitness goals. They're magic wands for health-conscious foodies! But there's one little hiccup that many of us have experienced in the waiting game with a single-basket air fryer.

If you have already been using an air fryer, you must have been in a situation where you're preparing a meal, and you want to cook both fries and chicken nuggets, but your trusty single-basket air fryer can only handle one at a time. It can be quite frustrating, right? You patiently wait for one item to finish cooking before popping in the next one. We've been there, too, and we understand the struggle.

That's where the "Tower Dual Basket Air Fryer" comes to the rescue, solving this common kitchen dilemma. Imagine having not one but two baskets in your air fryer! With this culinary powerhouse, you can simultaneously whip up two of your favorite dishes, saving time and energy. No more waiting around while your cravings grow stronger. This is a game-changer for everyone who loves delicious, healthy food without the wait.

This recipe book will show you how to make the most of your Tower Dual Basket Air Fryer. We'll take you on a culinary journey filled with scrumptious and nutritious recipes that are easy to follow and tailored to make the most of this fantastic appliance. Whether you're a novice in the kitchen or a seasoned chef, you'll find inspiration in these pages.

## About Tower Your Kitchen's Best Friend

Before we walk you through the delicious recipes, let's get to know the brand behind this kitchen marvel - Tower. Tower has been a trusted name in the world of kitchen appliances for over a century. The company has always strived to make our daily kitchen tasks more convenient and enjoyable. They understand our everyday challenges and work tirelessly to create solutions that make our lives easier.

The Tower Dual Basket Air Fryer is no exception to their mission. It's the result of innovative thinking and an unwavering commitment to quality. The Tower team has taken the time to listen to home chefs like you and me, identifying the issues we face with single-basket air fryers. They've turned those challenges into opportunities, bringing us a kitchen companion that simplifies our cooking adventures.

## Your Recipe Book Guide

Now that you're acquainted with the Tower Dual Basket Air Fryer and its incredible benefits, it's time to explore the heart of this recipe book - the recipes themselves. We've carefully curated a collection of delectable dishes catering to various tastes and dietary preferences.

Whether you're craving crispy classics like French fries or chicken wings or in the mood for something more exotic, such as coconut shrimp or teriyaki salmon, we've got you covered. And for our health-conscious readers, we haven't forgotten about you either! You'll find recipes that are low in calories, packed with nutrients, and flavorful.

Each recipe is designed with simplicity in mind. We understand that not everyone has hours to spend in the kitchen, so we've made sure that our recipes are easy to follow, with step-by-step instructions and clear ingredient lists. Even if you're new to air frying, you'll quickly become a pro with the help of this book.

## Your Fitness Journey Awaits with Convenience

As you flip through these pages, you'll discover that cooking with the Tower Dual Basket Air Fryer is an adventure waiting to happen. You'll become the master of your kitchen, impressing your family and friends with your culinary skills.

We encourage you to get creative and make each recipe your own. Feel free to add your favorite seasonings, swap out ingredients to suit your taste, and experiment with different cooking times to achieve your preferred level of crispiness. Cooking should be fun, and with the Tower Dual Basket Air Fryer, it's never been easier to let your creativity shine.

Throughout this recipe book, you'll find recipes bound to become family favorites, and your guests will be begging for your cooking secrets. Thanks to the Tower Dual Basket Air Fryer, you'll also find the satisfaction that comes with cooking delicious meals with ease.

First, we'll provide you with all the essential details about the Tower Dual Basket Air Fryer, ensuring that you're well-acquainted with this marvelous appliance before we dive into the delightful recipes. So, let's get started!

## Advantages of Using a Dual Basket Air Fryer

Let us tell you how magically it will change your cooking game. The Tower Dual Basket Air Fryer is more than just a kitchen gadget; it's a game-changer that offers many advantages that will transform how you prepare and enjoy your favorite meals. In this section, we will unravel the remarkable benefits of using a dual-basket air fryer like the Tower so you can truly appreciate the magic it brings to your kitchen.

# 1. Double the Capacity, Half the Wait

One of the most significant advantages of using a dual-basket air fryer is the ability to cook two different dishes simultaneously. Gone are the days of waiting for one item to finish cooking before you can start on the next. With the Tower Dual Basket Air Fryer, you can save time and effort by preparing a complete meal in one go. Crispy fries and tender chicken wings? No problem. Your meal will be ready in a fraction of the time it would take with a single-basket air fryer.

# 2. Healthier Cooking with Less Oil

If you're on a journey to healthier eating, a dual-basket air fryer is your ally. The Tower Dual Basket Air Fryer uses the power of hot air circulation to cook food, eliminating the need for excessive amounts of oil. You can enjoy all the crispy goodness of fried dishes with significantly less fat, making it a healthier alternative to traditional deep frying. It's a win-win situation, allowing you to indulge in your favorite comfort foods while making nutritious choices.

# 3. Improved Meal Planning

Dual basket air fryers like the Tower model offer greater flexibility regarding meal planning. You can easily prepare dishes with different cooking times and temperatures without worrying about cross-contamination of flavors. For instance, you can cook delicate fish fillets in one basket while crisping up some veggies in the other. This versatility is a game-changer, allowing you to experiment with a wider range of recipes and ingredients.

# 4. Energy-Efficient and Eco-Friendly

In today's world, energy efficiency and sustainability are essential considerations. The Tower Dual Basket Air Fryer is designed with these principles in mind. It consumes less energy than traditional ovens and stovetops, making it a greener option for cooking. Reducing energy consumption saves money on utility bills and contributes to a more sustainable environment.

# 5. Easy to Use and Beginner-Friendly

Cooking should be a joy, not a chore. Tower understands that not everyone is a professional chef, so their dual-basket air fryer is designed to be user-friendly. The controls are straightforward, and the display is easy to read, ensuring that even beginners can use it confidently. Say goodbye to kitchen intimidation and hello to a hassle-free cooking experience.

## 6. Perfect Crispiness Every Time

Achieving that ideal level of crispiness is an art, and the Tower Dual Basket Air Fryer helps you easily master it. The hot air circulates evenly around the food in both baskets, ensuring that every bite is perfectly crispy. Whether frying chicken, roasting vegetables, or baking pastries, you can count on consistent, mouthwatering results.

## 7. Multifunctional Versatility

The Tower Dual Basket Air Fryer is not limited to frying alone. It's a versatile kitchen companion that can handle various cooking tasks. This appliance can do everything from reheating leftovers to roasting, baking, and dehydrating. You can experiment with new recipes and cooking techniques by expanding your culinary repertoire.

## 8. Perfect for Entertaining

The dual-basket air fryer is your secret weapon if you love hosting gatherings and dinner parties. It lets you simultaneously whip up various appetizers and main courses, ensuring your guests have a delicious feast without long wait times. Whether it's game day or a special celebration, this appliance makes entertaining a breeze.

## 9. Reduces Meal Prep Stress

Life can get hectic, and preparing meals can be a source of stress. With a dual basket air fryer like the Tower, you can reduce the time and effort it takes to cook, leaving you more time to relax or spend with loved ones. Say goodbye to the dinner rush and hello to enjoyable, stress-free meal preparation.

## 10. Perfect for Families

For families, the Tower Dual Basket Air Fryer is a game-changer. You can accommodate various tastes and dietary preferences by cooking different dishes simultaneously. It's a versatile solution that ensures everyone at the table gets their favorite meal without a long wait, making family dinners more enjoyable and harmonious.

# Understanding the Tower Dual Basket Air Fryer: Easy and Iconic Cooking

The Tower Dual Basket Air Fryer is a culinary wonder and incredibly easy to use. Let's explore this fantastic kitchen appliance's user-friendly features and delve into its iconic language, making cooking a breeze for everyone, regardless of their experience in the kitchen.

## Smart Finish - Cooking Different Foods Together

Imagine you want to cook various foods together in your Tower Dual Basket Air Fryer, but they each have different cooking times and temperatures. That's where the Smart Finish function comes in handy. It's like having a kitchen magician! You can put one food item in each basket, and set the time and temperature for each, and the air fryer will ensure they're both perfectly cooked and ready simultaneously. First, you'll need to press "smart finish" and then set the temperature for both drawers. No more juggling or waiting around - it's cooking made smart and simple!

## Match Cook - Cooking the Same Food Twice

Sometimes, you want to cook the same delicious dish in both drawers. It's like making double the goodness. Here's where the Match Cook function shines. First, press match cook and then set the time and temperature to be applied on both drawers. It's a quick and easy way to get the same tasty results in both baskets, doubling your delight without the extra effort.

## Start/Pause - Getting the Cooking Started

Press the start button to kick off the cooking adventure with your Tower Dual Basket Air Fryer. It's as simple as that! After you've selected the right function, set the time, and adjusted the temperature, hit the start button, and the magic begins. If you need to pause the cooking process, press it again - cooking on your terms, without any fuss.

## Manually Setting the Temperature - Total Control at Your Fingertips

Now, let's talk about having total control over the temperature. Your Tower Dual Basket Air Fryer allows you to set the temperature just how you like it, from 50°C to 200°C. It's like having a thermostat for your cooking. To adjust the temperature, you can use the temperature adjustment keys. Each press increases or decreases the temperature by 10°C. If you keep pressing up and reach the maximum temperature of 200°C, don't worry! The air fryer is smart enough to loop back to 50°C if you press the "+" key again. You can make small changes with short presses or quickly change it by holding the adjustment keys. It's all about having the freedom to cook your way.

## Simplicity at Its Best: Easy to Use

One of the standout features of the Tower Dual Basket Air Fryer is its user-friendliness. Whether you're a seasoned chef or someone just beginning to explore the world of cooking, this appliance is designed to make your cooking process as straightforward as possible. There's no need to decipher complex controls or navigate through confusing menus. Instead, the Tower Dual Basket Air Fryer uses icons to guide you through cooking, making it a kitchen companion anyone can master.

## Iconic Language: Making Cooking Effortless

The Tower Dual Basket Air Fryer utilizes a set of intuitive icons that represent various cooking functions. These icons eliminate the need for complicated language or extensive user manuals. With a glance at the control panel, you'll clearly understand how to operate your air fryer, whether you want to fry, bake, grill, or even dehydrate. Let's take a closer look at some of the key icons and their meanings:

With these intuitive icons, the Tower Dual Basket Air Fryer simplifies your cooking experience, making it accessible to everyone. There's no need to memorize complicated instructions or spend hours learning how to use the appliance. Select the icon corresponding to your desired dish, and the air fryer will take care of the rest, ensuring your meals turn out just how you like them. Its cooking is made easy, all thanks to the iconic language of the Tower Dual Basket Air Fryer.

**1. Pre-Heat Icon:** This setting initiates a 3-minute warm-up phase at 180°C, ensuring the air fryer reaches the desired temperature before cooking begins, optimizing the overall cooking process.

**2. French Fries Icon:** Designed for to get crisp, this icon directs a cooking time of 18 minutes at 200°C, yielding crispy exteriors and fluffy interiors for the classic French fry texture.

**3. Drumsticks Icon:** This setting recommends a 20-minute cooking time at 200°C, guaranteeing a succulent and well-cooked result with a delightful crispy skin.

**4. Steak Icon:** The Steak icon specifies a 12-minute cooking duration at 180°C, striking a balance between achieving a savory sear on the outside and maintaining a juicy interior.

**5. Cake Icon:** This icon guides users through a 25-minute baking process at 160°C, ensuring cakes emerge from the air fryer with a moist and evenly cooked consistency.

**6. Shrimp Icon:** Suited for seafood lovers, this icon suggests an 8-minute cooking time at 180°C, resulting in perfectly cooked and slightly crispy shrimp, capturing the essence of delightful seafood cuisine.

**7. Fish Icon:** Fish icon prescribes a 10-minute cooking duration at 180°C, providing a quick and efficient method for achieving a tender, flaky texture.

**8. Pizza Icon:** Crafted for perfection, this setting recommends a 20-minute air frying process at 180°C, ensuring a crispy crust and evenly melted toppings for a delicious homemade pizza.

**9. Vegetables Icon:** Geared towards light dishes, this icon advises a 10-minute cooking time at 160°C, facilitating the roasting of vegetables to perfection, preserving both flavor and nutrients.

**10. Dehydrate Icon:** For those looking to preserve and intensify flavors, this icon signals a 6-hour dehydration process at 60°C, allowing users to create their own dried fruits, herbs, or snacks with ease.

# Maintaining Your Tower Dual Basket Air Fryer:
## A Breeze of a Task

Taking care of your Tower Dual Basket Air Fryer is as easy as cooking. Following a few simple maintenance steps, you can keep your appliance in great condition and ensure it continues serving you with delicious, crispy meals. Here's a quick guide to help you keep your air fryer in top shape:

### 1. Regular Cleaning

Cleaning is the key to keeping your air fryer in pristine condition. After each use, unplug it and allow it to cool down. Then, remove the baskets and trays for cleaning. They're usually dishwasher safe, but you can also wash them by hand with warm, soapy water. Wipe down the interior with a damp cloth or sponge. Be sure also to clean the heating element, which can accumulate oil and food particles. A clean air fryer not only looks better but also works better.

## 2. Preventing Buildup

Consider using a liner or parchment paper in the baskets to prevent stubborn buildup, like baked-on grease and food residue. This not only eases cleaning but also extends the life of your air fryer. Additionally, you can apply a small amount of cooking oil to the food to minimize sticking. It's a small step that goes a long way in maintenance.

## 3. Regular Inspections

Regularly give your air fryer a quick once-over to ensure no loose parts or visible damage. Check the power cord for any signs of wear and tear. Safety is paramount, so contact the manufacturer for guidance or replacement parts if you notice any damage.

## 4. Storage

Store your Tower Dual Basket Air Fryer in a dry and cool place when not in use. Make sure it's protected from dust and moisture. Storing it properly ensures it's ready for action when you need it.

## 5. Cooking Odor Control

If you notice any lingering cooking odors in your air fryer, you can easily eliminate them. Place a small bowl of water with a splash of lemon juice or vinegar in the air fryer basket and run it at a low temperature for a few minutes. This helps refresh the interior and keep it smelling clean and pleasant.

## 6. Filter Maintenance

Some air fryer models have built-in air filters. Check your user manual to see if your Tower Dual Basket Air Fryer has one. If it does, clean or replace the filter as the manufacturer recommends. This helps maintain the air quality and ensures optimal performance.

Following these straightforward maintenance tips, you can enjoy many more years of delicious, healthy cooking with your Tower Dual Basket Air Fryer. A little care goes a long way in preserving the magic of this kitchen marvel.

# You're Ready to Cook

Now that you've learned about the incredible Tower Dual Basket Air Fryer and how to maintain it, you're all set to embark on a delightful culinary adventure. The possibilities in your kitchen are endless, and it's time to let your inner chef shine.

Don't be disheartened by any initial failed attempts - every chef, seasoned or just starting, faces challenges. Cooking is a skill that takes time and practice to perfect. It's a journey filled with experimentation, learning, and, most importantly, the joy of creating delicious dishes.

When you step into the kitchen with your Tower Dual Basket Air Fryer, remember that it's perfectly okay to make mistakes. Those early mishaps are part of the learning process. They teach you what works and doesn't, helping you refine your culinary skills.

Don't be discouraged if a dish doesn't turn out as expected. Instead, use it as an opportunity to understand where you can make improvements. Perhaps you need to adjust the cooking time, temperature, or seasoning. Maybe you'll discover new ingredients and flavor combinations you hadn't considered before. Each setback is a step toward culinary mastery.

As you continue experimenting and honing your air frying skills, your confidence will grow, and your meals become more delicious. You'll develop your cooking style and preferences, creating dishes that are uniquely your own.

So, enjoy the journey if you plan to prepare a classic dish or explore new and exciting recipes. Have fun, be patient, and don't be afraid to push the boundaries of your culinary creativity. Remember, it's not about achieving perfection on your first try; it's about the joy of cooking and the satisfaction of sharing wonderful meals with your loved ones. Keep trying and learning, and you'll succeed. The Tower Dual Basket Air Fryer is here to help. Don't worry if you make mistakes at first; that's how we learn. With time, you'll become a great cook. So, let's not wait any longer - it's time to start cooking and enjoy some tasty recipes.

# Breakfast Recipes

# Crispy Bacon and Hash Brown with Eggs

*Cooking Period: 15 mins / Serving Portions: 2*
*Per Serving: Calories 285, Carbs 30.1g, Fat 10.5g, Protein 14.2g*

# Grilled Tomatoes and Crispy Mushrooms

*Cooking Period: 20 mins / Serving Portions: 2*
*Per Serving: Calories 315, Carbs 32g, Fat 14g, Protein 32g*

## Ingredients:

**For Bacon**
- Streaky bacon - 200g
- Salt and black pepper - to taste

**For Hash Browns with Egg**
- Potatoes peeled and grated -2 large
- Onion, finely chopped - 1 small
- Egg - 1 large
- Salt and black pepper - to taste

**For Serving**
- Fried eggs - 2

## Instructions:

1. Preheat your Tower Dual Basket Air Fryer by pressing the "Pre-Heat" icon, which looks like a wave icon, and set the temperature to 200°C using the temperature adjustment keys. Wait for 3 minutes until it's ready.
2. Mix the grated potatoes, chopped onion, and egg for the hash browns in a bowl. Season the mixture with a pinch of salt and black pepper.
3. Shape the potato mixture into hash brown patties.
4. It's time to use the Air fryer; lay the streaky bacon strips in a single layer in the "left drawer" of the air fryer.
5. Now, place the hash brown patties in the "right drawer" of the air fryer.
6. Cook the bacon at 200°C by pressing the "Steak" icon and set the time to 10 minutes. Adjust the cooking time if you prefer your bacon to be crispier.
7. Cook the hash browns at 180°C by pressing the "Vegetable" icon, and set the time to 15 minutes.
8. It's time to serve once the bacon and hash browns are done. Place some crispy bacon beside the hash brown patties. Add a sunny-side-up egg onto each plate.
9. Tap on "Smart Finish" to ensure they are ready simultaneously.
10. You're ready to enjoy the tasty mix of flavors and textures. If you want, sprinkle more salt and black pepper for extra flavor.

## Ingredients:

**For Grilled Tomatoes**
- Tomatoes - 3 large, ripped
- Olive oil - 40 ml
- Salt and black pepper - to taste
- Fresh thyme leaves - 1g

**For Crispy Mushrooms**
- Button mushrooms - 200g
- Olive oil - 10 ml
- Garlic powder - 5g
- Paprika - 5g
- Salt and black pepper - to taste

## Instructions:

1. To prepare your Tower Dual Basket Air Fryer, press the "Preheat" button and choose 180°C for the temperature. Wait for 3 minutes until it's heated and ready.
2. While the air fryer is preheating, cut the tomatoes in half and place them in a bowl. Drizzle with olive oil, and season with salt, black pepper, and fresh thyme leaves. Toss to coat the tomatoes evenly.
3. In a separate bowl, clean and quarter the button mushrooms. Drizzle them with olive oil and season with garlic powder, paprika, salt, and black pepper. Toss to coat the mushrooms evenly.
4. Lay the seasoned tomato halves in a single layer in the "left drawer" of the air fryer.
5. Place the seasoned mushroom quarters in the "right drawer" of the air fryer.
6. Tap on "Match Cook" to cook them at the same time and temperature.
7. Cook them at 180°C by pressing the "Vegetables" icon and wait 10 minutes.
8. It's time to serve once the grilled tomatoes and crispy mushrooms are done. Arrange the tomatoes and mushrooms on a plate and garnish with extra thyme leaves for the tomatoes and a sprinkle of paprika for the mushrooms.

# Apple Muffins

*Cooking Period: 20 mins / Serving Portions: 8*
*Per Serving: Calories 398, Carbs 35g, Fat 25.8g, Protein 5.6g*

**Ingredients:**

- All-purpose flour - 130g
- Baking powder - 1g
- Butter - 225g, softened
- Vanilla extract - 2½ml
- Rolled oats - 50g
- Powdered sugar - 130g
- Eggs - 4
- Raisins - 80g

**Instructions:**

1. In a bowl, mix together the flour, oats, and baking powder.
2. In another bowl, add the sugar and butter and whisk until creamy.
3. Then, add in the egg and vanilla extract and whisk until well combined.
4. Add the egg mixture into oat mixture and mix until just combined.
5. Fold in the raisins.
6. Place the mixture into 8 greased muffin molds evenly.
7. Preheat your Tower Dual Basket Air Fryer using the "Pre-Heat" icon at 180°C and wait for 3 minutes.
8. Place the muffin molds into both drawers.
9. Use the "Match Cook" icon to set the same time and temperature for both drawers, 20 minutes at 160°C, using the "Cake" icon.
10. Press "Start" to begin cooking.
11. Once done, transfer the muffin molds onto a wire rack to cool for about 10 minutes.
12. Carefully invert the muffins onto the wire rack to completely cool before serving.

# Banana Walnut Muffins

*Cooking Period: 20 mins / Serving Portions: 8*
*Per Serving: Calories 9, Carbs 24.6g, Fat 14g, Protein 3g*

**Ingredients:**

- Oats - 50g
- Refined flour - 70g
- Baking powder - 4g
- Unsalted butter - 110g, softened
- Powdered sugar - 70g
- Whole milk - 10ml
- Banana - 75g, peeled and mashed
- Vanilla extract - 5ml
- Walnuts - 30g, chopped

**Instructions:**

1. In a bowl, mix together the oats, flour and baking powder.
2. In another bowl, add the sugar and butter and beat until creamy
3. Add the banana and vanilla extract and beat until well combined.
4. Add the flour mixture and milk in banana mixture and mix until just combined.
5. Fold in the walnuts.
6. Grease 8 muffin molds with baking spray.
7. Place the mixture into the prepared muffin molds evenly.
8. Preheat your Tower Dual Basket Air Fryer using the "Pre-Heat" icon at 180°C and wait for 3 minutes.
9. Place the muffin molds into both drawers.
10. Use the "Match Cook" function to set the same time and temperature for both drawers, 20 minutes at 160°C, using the "Cake" icon.
11. Press "Start" to begin cooking.
12. Once done, remove the muffin molds from Air Fryer and place onto a wire rack to cool for about 10 minutes.
13. Carefully invert the muffins onto wire rack to completely cool before serving.

# Veggie-Filled Frittata with Sweet Potato Hash Browns

*Cooking Period: 25 mins / Serving Portions: 2*
*Per Serving: Calories 320, Carbs 30g, Fat 16g, Protein 15g*

# Zucchini Bread

*Cooking Period: 25 mins / Serving Portions: 16*
*Per Serving: Calories 367, Carbs 47.4g, Fat 18.6g, Protein 5.2g*

## Ingredients:

**For Veggie-Filled Frittata**
- Eggs - 6 Large
- Zucchini - 240 g
- Cherry tomatoes - 240 g
- Red bell pepper - 1 diced
- Red onion - 1 diced
- Fresh basil leaves - 30 ml
- Olive oil - 30 ml
- Salt - to taste
- Black pepper - to taste

**For Sweet Potato Hash Browns:**
- Sweet potatoes - 2 medium
- Olive oil - 30 ml
- Salt and black pepper - to taste

## Instructions:

1. Preheat your Tower Dual Basket Air Fryer to 180°C.
2. In the "right drawer," add the diced zucchini, cherry tomatoes, red bell pepper, and red onion. Drizzle with olive oil and season with salt and black pepper.
3. In the "left drawer." place the grated sweet potatoes for the hash browns. Drizzle with olive oil and season with salt and black pepper.
4. Tap on "Match Cook" and cook at 180°C using the "Vegetables" icon for 15 minutes.
5. Whisk the eggs in a bowl while the vegetables and hash browns cook, and stir in the chopped basil. Season with salt and black pepper.
6. Once the vegetables and hash browns are done, combine them in a baking dish and pour the egg mixture over the top.
7. Cook the frittata at 180°C using the "Vegetables" icon for 10 minutes.
8. Slice the frittata into wedges and serve with the sweet potato hash browns.
9. Enjoy your veggie-filled breakfast frittata with sweet potato hash browns!

## Ingredients:

- All-purpose flour - 360g
- Baking soda - 4g
- Baking powder - 4g
- Ground cinnamon - 10g
- Salt - 5g
- White sugar - 450g
- Vegetable oil - 240ml
- Eggs - 3
- Vanilla extract - 15ml
- Zucchini - 350g, grated
- Walnuts - 100g, chopped

## Instructions:

1. In a bowl, mix together the flour, baking powder, baking soda, cinnamon, and salt.
2. In another large bowl, add the sugar, oil, eggs, and vanilla extract and beat until well combined.
3. Then, add in the flour mixture and stir until just combined.
4. Gently fold in the zucchini and walnuts.
5. Grease 2 (8x4-inch) loaf pans and then dust each with a little flour.
6. Place the mixture into the prepared pans evenly.
7. Preheat your Tower Dual Basket Air Fryer using the "Pre-Heat" icon at 180°C and wait for 3 minutes.
8. Place 1 loaf pan into each drawers.
9. Use the "Match Cook" function to set the same time and temperature for both drawers, 25 minutes at 160°C, using the "Cake" icon.
10. Press "Start" to begin cooking.
11. Once done, remove the pans from Air Fryer and place onto a wire rack for about 10-15 minutes.
12. Carefully remove the breads from each pan and place onto the wire rack to cool completely before slicing.
13. Cut each bread into desired sized slices and serve.

# Banana Bread

*Cooking Period: 22 mins / Serving Portions: 16*
*Per Serving: Calories 301, Carbs 41.1g, Fat 14.9g, Protein 3.6g*

## Ingredients:

- All-purpose flour - 400g
- White sugar - 170g
- Baking soda - 8g
- Baking powder - 8g
- Ground cinnamon - 10g
- Salt - 5g
- Whole milk - 240ml
- Olive oil - 240ml
- Bananas - 6, peeled and sliced

## Instructions:

1. In a bowl of a stand mixer, add all the ingredients and mix well.
2. Grease 2 loaf pans with baking spray.
3. Place the mixture into the loaf pans evenly.
4. Preheat your Tower Dual Basket Air Fryer using the "Pre-Heat" icon at 180°C and wait for 3 minutes.
5. Place 1 loaf pan into each drawers.
6. Use the "Match Cook" function to set the same time and temperature for both drawers, 22 minutes at 160°C, using the "Cake" icon.
7. Press "Start" to begin cooking.
8. Once done, remove the pans from Air Fryer and place onto a wire rack for about 10-15 minutes.
9. Carefully remove the breads from each pan and place onto the wire rack to cool completely before slicing.
10. Cut each bread into desired sized slices and serve.

# Salmon & Broccoli Quiche

*Cooking Period: 15 mins / Serving Portions: 8*
*Per Serving: Calories 196, Carbs 16.5g, Fat 12.3g, Protein 6.2g*

## Ingredients:

- Frozen ready-made pie crust - 1
- Olive oil - 10ml
- Egg - 1
- Cheddar cheese - 40g, grated
- Whipping cream - 60g
- Salt and ground black pepper - to taste
- Cooked broccoli - 25g, chopped
- Cooked salmon - 35g, chopped

## Instructions:

1. Lightly, grease 2 small pie pans with olive oil.
2. Cut 2 (5-inch) rounds from the pie crust.
3. Arrange 1 pie crust round in each pie pan and gently, press in the bottom and sides.
4. In a bowl, mix together the egg, cheese, cream, salt, and black pepper.
5. Pour the egg mixture over dough base and top with broccoli and salmon.
6. Preheat your Tower Dual Basket Air Fryer using the "Pre-Heat" icon at 180°C and wait for 3 minutes.
7. Place 1 pie pan into each drawer.
8. Use the "Match Cook" function to Manually set the temperature at 180°C for 15 minutes.
9. Once done, remove the pans from Air Fryer and place onto a wire rack for about 5 minutes before serving.

# Green Veggies Frittata

*Cooking Period: 15 mins /Serving Portions: 4*
*Per Serving: Calories 278, Carbs 8g, Fat 19.4g, Protein 18.8g*

# Cheese & Cream Omelet

*Cooking Period: 20 mins /Serving Portions: 4*
*Per Serving: Calories 263, Carbs 4.6g, Fat 20.4g, Protein 15.8g*

## Ingredients:

- Half-and-half - 120g
- Large eggs - 8
- Salt and ground black pepper - as required
- Fresh kale - 120g, chopped
- Fresh spinach - 120g, chopped
- Onion - 120g, chopped
- Feta cheese - 110g, crumbled

## Instructions:

1. In a bowl, add the half-and-half, eggs, salt and black pepper and beat until well combined.
2. Add the spinach, kale, onion and feta cheese and mix well.
3. Place the mixture into two baking pans evenly.
4. Preheat your Tower Dual Basket Air Fryer using the "Pre-Heat" icon at 180°C and wait for 3 minutes.
5. Place 1 pan into each drawer.
6. Use the "Match Cook" function to manually set the temperature at 180°C for 20 minutes.
7. Once done, remove the pans from Air Fryer and place onto a wire rack for about 5 minutes before serving.

## Ingredients:

- Eggs - 8
- Cream - 120g
- Salt and ground black pepper - as required
- Cheddar cheese - 60g, grated

## Instructions:

1. Lightly grease 2 small baking pans.
2. In a bowl, add the eggs, cream, salt, and black pepper and beat until well combined.
3. Place the egg mixture into both prepared pans.
4. Preheat your Tower Dual Basket Air Fryer using the "Pre-Heat" icon at 180°C and wait for 3 minutes.
5. Place 1 pan into each drawer.
6. Use the "Match Cook" function to manually set the temperature at 180°C for 8 minutes.
7. After 4 minutes of cooking, sprinkle the cheese on the top of omelet in each pan.
8. Once done, remove the pans from Air Fryer and place onto a wire rack for about 5 minutes before serving.

# Baked Cod with Roasted Vegetables

*Cooking Period: 20 mins / Serving Portions: 2*
*Per Serving: Calories 250, Carbs 10g, Fat 8g, Protein 30g*

**Ingredients:**

- Fresh cod fillets - 2 (200g each)
- Sweet potatoes - 300g, sliced into thin rounds
- Courgettes (zucchini) - 2, sliced
- Red bell pepper - 1, sliced
- Olive oil - 30ml
- Lemon - 1, sliced
- Salt - to taste
- Black pepper - to taste
- Paprika - 3g

**Instructions:**

1. To get your Tower Dual Basket Air Fryer ready for cooking, choose the "Pre-Heat" option and let it heat up for about 3 minutes until it's ready for use.
2. In the "left drawer" of the air fryer, place the sliced sweet potatoes, courgettes, and red bell pepper. Drizzle with olive oil and season with salt, black pepper, and paprika. Toss to coat.
3. In the "right drawer" of the air fryer, season the cod fillets with a pinch of salt and black pepper. Place lemon slices on top of the fillets.
4. Use the "Smart Finish" icon with the "Fish" icon for the pork in the left drawer and set at 180°C for 8 minutes.
5. Use the "Vegetables" icon for the bell veggie mixture in the right drawer and set at 160°C for 10 minutes. Press "Start" to begin cooking.
6. Once the cod and vegetables are done, it's time to serve. Arrange the roasted vegetables on a plate and place the cod fillet on top.
7. Serve hot with a squeeze of fresh lemon juice, and enjoy this healthy and flavourful meal.

# Beef Taco Rolls

*Cooking Period: 8 mins / Serving Portions: 6*
*Per Serving: Calories 880, Carbs 42.6g, Fat 58.9g, Protein 65.5g*

**Ingredients:**

- Flour tortillas - 6
- Cooked ground beef - 910g
- Nacho cheese - 340g
- Tostadas - 6
- Sour cream - 480g
- Bibb lettuce - 150g, shredded
- Roma tomatoes - 3, sliced
- Mexican blend cheese - 230g, shredded
- Olive oil cooking spray

**Instructions:**

1. Arrange the tortillas onto a smooth surface.
2. Place the beef in the center of each tortilla evenly, followed by the nacho cheese, tostada, sour cream, lettuce, tomato slices and Mexican cheese.
3. Bring the edges of each tortilla up, over the center to look like a pinwheel.
4. To get your Tower Dual Basket Air Fryer ready, activate the "Preheat" icon and let it warm up for around 3 minutes.
5. Place the rolls into both drawers.
6. Use the "Match Cook" icon and manually set the temperature at 200°C for 8 minutes.
7. Press "Start" to begin cooking.
8. Once done, serve the rolls warm.

# Beef and Vegetable Skewers

*Cooking Period: 12 mins / Serving Portions: 4*
*Per Serving: Calories 280, Carbs 10g, Fat 12g, Protein 35g*

**Ingredients:**

- Beef sirloin steaks - 4 (200g each), cubed
- Bell peppers (red, green, and yellow) - 4 diced
- Red onion - 2, diced
- Cherry tomatoes - 24
- Olive oil - 60ml
- Paprika - 5g
- Garlic powder - 5g
- Salt - to taste
- Black pepper - to taste
- Wooden skewers - soaked in water

**Instructions:**

1. Thread the cubed beef, bell peppers, red onion, and cherry tomatoes onto the soaked wooden skewers. Drizzle with olive oil and season with paprika, garlic powder, salt, and black pepper.
2. Preheat your Tower Dual Basket Air Fryer using the "Pre-Heat" icon at 180°C and wait for 3 minutes.
3. Place the skewers into both drawers.
4. Use the "Match Cook" icon to set the same time and temperature for both drawers, 12 minutes at 180°C, using the "Steak" icon.
5. Press "Start" to begin cooking.
6. Serve hot with a side of your favorite dipping sauce, and enjoy these delicious beef and vegetable skewers, perfect for a healthy lunch.

# Quinoa and Vegetable Stuffed Bell Peppers

*Cooking Period: 25 mins | Serving Portions: 2*
*Per Serving: Calories 300, Carbs 40g, Fat 10g, Protein 10g*

**Ingredients:**

- Bell peppers (red, green, or yellow) - 4
- Quinoa - 200g
- Cherry tomatoes -150g, halved
- Baby spinach - 30g
- Red onion - 1, finely chopped
- Olive oil - 30ml
- Lemon juice - 30ml
- Paprika - 3g
- Salt - to taste
- Black pepper - to taste

**Instructions:**

1. Get your Tower Dual Basket Air Fryer ready by pressing "Preheat" and setting it to 160°C. Wait for 3 minutes, and it will be good to go.
2. In the "left drawer" of the air fryer, cut the tops off the bell peppers and remove the seeds. Place the bell peppers in the drawer.
3. Mix cherry tomatoes, baby spinach, red onion, olive oil, lemon juice, paprika, salt, and black pepper in a mixing bowl. Mix well.
4. Once the quinoa is cooked, stir it into the vegetable mixture.
5. Stuff the cooked quinoa and vegetable mixture into the bell peppers in the "left drawer."
6. Both require the same cooking time and temperature: 10 minutes at 160°C.
7. Press "Match cook" and then select the vegetable icon to start.
8. Serve hot, and enjoy these delicious quinoa and vegetable-stuffed bell peppers.

# Grilled Cheese and Tomato Sandwich

*Cooking Period: 10 mins / Serving Portions: 2*
*Per Serving: Calories 350, Carbs 30g, Fat 18g, Protein 15g*

## Ingredients:

- Whole-grain bread - 4 slices
- Cheddar cheese - 4 slices
- Tomato - 1, thinly sliced
- Butter - 30ml
- Salt - to taste
- Black pepper - to taste

## Instructions:

1. Preheat your Tower Dual Basket Air Fryer by pressing the "Preheat" icon and set the temperature to 180°C. Wait for 3 minutes until it's ready.
2. In the "left drawer" of the air fryer, lay out 2 slices of whole-grain bread.
3. Top each slice with a slice of cheddar cheese and tomato slices.
4. Place the remaining slices of whole-grain bread on top to form sandwiches.
5. Place the sandwiches in the "right drawer" of the air fryer.
6. Spread a little butter on the top of each sandwich.
7. Manually set the temperature at 180°C for 10 minutes.
8. After 5 minutes, flip the sandwiches, spread the remaining butter on the other side.
9. Serve hot with a side salad, and enjoy a classic grilled cheese and tomato sandwich.

# Sweet Potato and Chickpea Curry

*Cooking Period: 25 mins / Serving Portions: 2*
*Per Serving: Calories 320, Carbs 50g, Fat 8g, Protein 10g*

## Ingredients:

- Sweet potatoes - 2, peeled and diced
- Chickpeas - 400g, drained and rinsed
- Onion - 1, finely chopped
- Garlic - 2 cloves, minced
- Ginger - 1-inch piece, grated
- Curry powder -20g
- Coconut milk - 400ml
- Olive oil - 30ml
- Salt - to taste
- Black pepper - to taste
- Fresh coriander - for garnish

## Instructions:

1. To get your Tower Dual Basket Air Fryer ready, press the "Preheat" icon and wait 3 minutes.
2. In the "left drawer" of the air fryer, place the diced sweet potatoes, chickpeas, chopped onion, minced garlic, and grated ginger. Drizzle with olive oil, sprinkle curry powder, salt, and black pepper. Toss to coat.
3. Cook the curry in the "left drawer" at 180°C using the "Vegetables" icon for 10 minutes.
4. Once the curry is done, it's time to serve.
5. Serve hot with a garnish of fresh coriander, and enjoy a hearty and spicy sweet potato and chickpea curry.

# Tofu and Vegetable Stir-Fry

*Cooking Period: 20 mins /Serving Portions: 2*
*Per Serving: Calories 250, Carbs 20g, Fat 10g, Protein 20g*

## Ingredients:

- Tofu - 1 block, cubed
- Broccoli florets - 200g
- Red bell pepper - 1, sliced
- Snow peas - 100g
- Carrots - 2, thinly sliced
- Soy sauce - 30ml
- Sesame oil - 15ml
- Ginger - 1-inch piece, grated
- Garlic - 2 cloves, minced
- Olive oil - 30ml
- Salt - to taste
- Black pepper - to taste

## Instructions:

1. Begin the preheating process of your Tower Dual Basket Air Fryer by selecting the "Pre-Heat" icon. Allow it to preheat for 3 minutes until it reaches the desired temperature.
2. Place the cubed tofu in the air fryer's "left drawer" and drizzle with olive oil.
3. In the "right drawer" of the air fryer, place the broccoli florets, red bell pepper, snow peas, and sliced carrots. Drizzle with olive oil, season with salt and black pepper.
4. Press the "Match Cook" icon and set both drawers to cook at 180°C using the "Vegetables" icon for 10 minutes.
5. While the tofu and vegetables are cooking, make the stir-fry sauce by combining soy sauce, sesame oil, grated ginger, and minced garlic in a bowl.
6. Once the tofu and vegetables are cooked, combine them in a large bowl and pour the stir-fry sauce over them.
7. Serve hot, and enjoy this healthy and flavourful tofu and vegetable stir-fry.

# Spinach and Mushroom Stuffed Chicken Breast

*Cooking Period: 25 mins /Serving Portions: 2*
*Per Serving: Calories 350, Carbs 10g, Fat 15g, Protein 40g*

## Ingredients:

- Chicken breasts - 2 (200g each)
- Spinach - 60g
- Button mushrooms - 200g, sliced
- Garlic - 2 cloves, minced
- Olive oil - 30ml
- Salt - to taste
- Black pepper - to taste
- Paprika - 3g

## Instructions:

1. To prepare your Tower Dual Basket Air Fryer, activate the "Pre-Heat" icon and patiently wait approximately 3 minutes.
2. In the "left drawer" of the air fryer, sauté the sliced mushrooms and minced garlic with olive oil. Season with salt, black pepper, and paprika.
3. Season the chicken breasts with salt and black pepper in the "right drawer" of the air fryer. Cut a pocket into each chicken breast.
4. Stuff each chicken breast with spinach.
5. Cook the vegetables in the left drawer for 10 minutes at 180°C using the "Vegetables" icon."
6. Cook the stuffed chicken breasts at 180°C by pressing the "Drumsticks" icon and set the time to 15 minutes.
7. Tap on "Smart Finish" to ensure both the mushrooms and chicken are ready at the same time.
8. Once the mushrooms and chicken are done, serve the chicken on a plate topped with sautéed mushrooms.
9. Serve hot and enjoy this delicious and nutritious spinach and mushroom-stuffed chicken breast.

# Beef Cheeseburgers

*Cooking Period: 11 mins / Serving Portions: 8*
*Per Serving: Calories 377, Carbs 14g, Fat 29.3g, Protein 17.5g*

**Ingredients:**

- Ground beef - 910g
- Garlic cloves - 4, minced
- Fresh cilantro - 15g, minced
- Salt and ground black pepper, as required
- Cheddar cheese slices - 8
- Large tomatoes - 4, sliced
- Large cucumbers - 3, sliced
- Large red onion - 1, sliced
- Lettuce heads - 4, torn
- Olive oil - 120ml
- Lemon juice - 60ml

**Instructions:**

1. In a bowl, mix together the beef, garlic, cilantro, salt, and black pepper.
2. Make 8 (4-inch) patties from the mixture.
3. Preheat your Tower Dual Basket Air Fryer using the "Pre-Heat" icon at 180°C and wait for 3 minutes.
4. Place the patties into both drawers.
5. Use the "Match Cook" icon to manually set the temperature at 180°C for 11 minutes.
6. After 5 minutes of cooking, flip the patties.
7. After 10 minutes of cooking, place 1 cheese slice over each patty.
8. Meanwhile, for the salad: in a large salad bowl, add tomatoes, cucumbers, onion, lettuce, oil, lemon juice, salt, and black pepper and toss to coat.
9. Once the patties are done, transfer them onto serving plates.
10. Enjoy alongside the salad as your filling lunch.

# Salmon and Asparagus Parcels

*Cooking Period: 25 mins / Serving Portions: 2*
*Per Serving: Calories 300, Carbs 10g, Fat 15g, Protein 30g*

**Ingredients:**

- Salmon fillets - 2 (200g each)
- Asparagus spears - 200g
- Lemon - 1, sliced
- Fresh dill - 2g, chopped
- Olive oil - 30ml
- Salt - to taste
- Black pepper - to taste
- Garlic - 2 cloves, minced

**Instructions:**

1. Preheat your Tower Dual Basket Air Fryer by pressing the "Preheat" icon and set the temperature to 180°C. Wait for 3 minutes until it's ready.
2. In the "left drawer" of the air fryer, lay out two large squares of aluminum foil.
3. Place the salmon fillets in the center of each foil square.
4. Arrange the asparagus spears around the salmon, and drizzle olive oil over the salmon and asparagus.
5. Season with salt, black pepper, and minced garlic.
6. Place lemon slices on each salmon fillet and sprinkle with chopped dill.
7. Fold the foil squares to create sealed parcels, ensuring no openings.
8. Use the "Smart Finish" icon with the "Fish" icon and set at 180°C for 15 minutes.
9. Use the "Vegetables" icon for the bell pepper mixture in the right drawer and set at 160°C for 10 minutes. Press "Start" to begin cooking.
10. Once the parcels are done, carefully open them and serve the salmon and asparagus hot.
11. Enjoy a delicious and healthy lunch with these flavourful salmon and asparagus parcels and a side salad if desired.

# Appetizers and Side Dishes

# Crispy Vegetable Spring Rolls

*Cooking Period: 15 mins / Serving Portions: 4*
*Per Serving: Calories 150, Carbs 12g, Fat 8g, Protein 5g*

**Ingredients:**

- Spring roll wrappers - 12 sheets
- Mixed vegetables (carrots, cabbage, and bell peppers) - 300g, julienned
- Bean sprouts - 100g
- Soy sauce - 30ml
- Sesame oil - 15ml
- Ground ginger - 5g
- Garlic - 2 cloves, minced
- Salt - to taste
- Black pepper - to taste

**Instructions:**

1. Combine the julienned vegetables, bean sprouts, soy sauce, sesame oil, ground ginger, minced garlic, salt, and black pepper in a bowl. Toss to mix well.
2. Place a spring roll wrapper on a clean surface. Add a portion of the vegetable mixture to the center and fold the sides. Roll it up tightly, sealing the edges with a bit of water.
3. To preheat your Tower Dual Basket Air Fryer, select the "Preheat" icon and patiently wait approximately 3 minutes until it reaches the desired temperature.
4. Place the spring rolls in the "left drawer" of the air fryer.
5. Cook them for 8 minutes using the "default" icon at 200°C.
6. Once the spring rolls are crispy and golden, serve them hot with a dipping sauce.

# Garlic Parmesan Zucchini Fries

*Cooking Period: 20 mins / Serving Portions: 4*
*Per Serving: Calories 120, Carbs 10g, Fat 7g, Protein 5g*

**Ingredients:**

- Zucchini - 400g, cut into sticks
- Parmesan cheese - 30g, grated
- Breadcrumbs - 30g
- Garlic powder - 5g
- Salt - to taste
- Black pepper - to taste
- Olive oil - 30ml

**Instructions:**

1. To prepare your Tower Dual Basket Air Fryer, select the "Preheat" icon and allow it to warm up for approximately 3 minutes.
2. Mix the grated Parmesan, breadcrumbs, garlic powder, salt, and black pepper in a shallow bowl.
3. Dip each zucchini stick into olive oil, then coat it with the breadcrumb mixture.
4. Place the coated zucchini sticks in the "left drawer" of the air fryer.
5. Press "Start/Pause" to cook them at 200°C using the "French Fries" icon and adjust the time to 12 minutes.
6. Once the zucchini fries are golden and crispy, serve them hot with a side of marinara sauce.

# Spinach Stuffed Mushrooms

*Cooking Period: 18 mins / Serving Portions: 4*
*Per Serving: Calories 80, Carbs 5g, Fat 6g, Protein 4g*

**Ingredients:**

- White mushrooms - 12 large
- Baby spinach - 150g
- Cream cheese - 60g
- Grated Parmesan cheese - 30g
- Garlic - 2 cloves, minced
- Olive oil - 30ml
- Salt - to taste
- Black pepper - to taste

**Instructions:**

1. To prepare your Tower Dual Basket Air Fryer for cooking, choose the "Preheat" setting and let it heat up for around 3 minutes.
2. Remove the stems from the mushrooms and chop them finely.
3. In a pan, sauté the chopped mushroom stems and minced garlic in olive oil until softened. Add the baby spinach and cook until wilted.
4. Mix the sautéed vegetables in a bowl with cream cheese, Parmesan cheese, salt, and black pepper.
5. Stuff each mushroom cap with the mixture.
6. Place the stuffed mushrooms in the "left drawer" of the air fryer.
7. Press "Start/Pause" to cook them at 180°C using the "Vegetables" icon for 10 minutes.
8. Once the stuffed mushrooms are golden and the filling is bubbly, serve them hot as a delicious appetizer.

# Sweet Potato and Carrot Fritters

*Cooking Period: 15 mins / Serving Portions: 4*
*Per Serving: Calories 120, Carbs 15g, Fat 5g, Protein 2g*

**Ingredients:**

- Sweet potatoes - 300g, grated
- Carrots - 200g, grated
- Red onion - 1, finely chopped
- Eggs - 2
- Whole wheat flour - 30g
- Paprika - 5g
- Cumin - 5g
- Salt - to taste
- Black pepper - to taste
- Olive oil - 30ml

**Instructions:**

1. To ready your Tower Dual Basket Air Fryer for operation, click on the "Preheat" icon and let it heat up for about 3 minutes.
2. Combine the grated sweet potatoes, carrots, finely chopped red onion, eggs, whole wheat flour, paprika, cumin, salt, and black pepper in a bowl.
3. Form the mixture into small patties and place them in the "left drawer" of the air fryer.
4. Press "Start/Pause" to cook the fritters at 180°C using the "Vegetables" icon for 10 minutes.
5. Once the fritters are crispy and golden, serve them hot with a dollop of Greek yogurt or a dipping sauce.

# Balsamic Roasted Brussels Sprouts

*Cooking Period: 12 mins* / *Serving Portions: 4*
*Per Serving: Calories 90, Carbs 10g, Fat 5g, Protein 3g*

**Ingredients:**

- Brussels sprouts - 400g, trimmed and halved
- Balsamic vinegar - 30ml
- Olive oil - 30ml
- Honey - 15ml
- Garlic - 2 cloves, minced
- Salt - to taste
- Black pepper - to taste

**Instructions:**

1. Preheat your Tower Dual Basket Air Fryer by pressing the "Preheat" icon and set the temperature to 180°C. Wait for 3 minutes until it's ready.
2. In a bowl, combine balsamic vinegar, olive oil, honey, minced garlic, salt, and black pepper.
3. Toss the halved Brussels sprouts in the balsamic mixture until they are well coated.
4. Place the coated Brussels sprouts in the "left drawer" of the air fryer.
5. Press "Start/Pause" to roast them at 180°C using the "Vegetables" icon and adjust the time to 12 minutes.
6. Once the Brussels sprouts are caramelized and tender, serve them hot as a delightful side dish.

# Crispy Kale Chips

*Cooking Period: 10 mins* / *Serving Portions: 4*
*Per Serving: Calories 50, Carbs 8g, Fat 3g, Protein 2g*

**Ingredients:**

- Fresh kale leaves - 200g, torn into bite-sized pieces
- Olive oil - 30ml
- Nutritional yeast - 20g
- Smoked paprika - 5g
- Salt - to taste
- Black pepper - to taste

**Instructions:**

1. To prepare your Tower Dual Basket Air Fryer for cooking, choose the "Preheat" option and let it heat up for around 3 minutes.
2. Toss the torn kale pieces with olive oil, nutritional yeast, smoked paprika, salt, and black pepper in a bowl.
3. Place the seasoned kale in the "left drawer" of the air fryer.
4. Press "Start/Pause" to cook them at 160°C using the "Vegetables" icon for 8 minutes.
5. Once the kale chips are crispy and lightly browned, serve them as a guilt-free and flavourful snack or side dish.

# Mozzarella-Stuffed Portobello Mushrooms

*Cooking Period: 15 mins / Serving Portions: 4*
*Per Serving: Calories 140, Carbs 7g, Fat 10g, Protein 7g*

## Ingredients:

- Portobello mushrooms - 4 large
- Fresh mozzarella cheese - 100g, sliced
- Cherry tomatoes - 150g, halved
- Fresh basil leaves - 10g
- Balsamic glaze - 30ml
- Olive oil - 30ml
- Garlic - 2 cloves, minced
- Salt - to taste
- Black pepper - to taste

## Instructions:

1. To ready your Tower Dual Basket Air Fryer for cooking, click on the "Preheat" symbol and let it warm up for about 3 minutes.
2. Remove the stems from the Portobello mushrooms and brush them with olive oil.
3. Stuff each mushroom with slices of fresh mozzarella, halved cherry tomatoes, minced garlic, and fresh basil leaves.
4. Place the stuffed mushrooms in the "left drawer" of the air fryer.
5. Press "Start/Pause" to cook them at 180°C using the "Vegetable" icon for 10 minutes.
6. Once the mushrooms are tender and the cheese is melted, drizzle with balsamic glaze and serve hot.

# Crispy Buffalo Cauliflower Bites

*Cooking Period: 20 mins / Serving Portions: 4*
*Per Serving: Calories 120, Carbs 10g, Fat 7g, Protein 5g*

## Ingredients:

- Cauliflower florets - 400g
- Buffalo hot sauce - 60ml
- Whole wheat flour - 30g
- Paprika - 5g
- Garlic powder - 5g
- Salt - to taste
- Black pepper - to taste
- Olive oil - 30ml

## Instructions:

1. To prepare your Tower Dual Basket Air Fryer for cooking, select the "Preheat" icon and allow it to heat up for approximately 3 minutes.
2. Combine whole wheat flour, paprika, garlic powder, salt, and black pepper in a bowl.
3. Dip each cauliflower floret into olive oil, then coat it with the flour mixture.
4. Place the coated cauliflower bites in the "left drawer" of the air fryer.
5. Press "Start/Pause" to cook them at 160°C using the "Vegetable" icon for 15 minutes.
6. Once the cauliflower bites are crispy, toss them in buffalo hot sauce and serve hot with a side of ranch dressing.

# Spiced Roasted Butternut Squash

*Cooking Period: 20 mins / Serving Portions: 4*
*Per Serving: Calories 80, Carbs 20g, Fat 1g, Protein 2g*

**Ingredients:**

- Butternut squash - 500g, peeled and cubed
- Ground cinnamon - 5g
- Ground cumin - 5g
- Ground coriander - 5g
- Olive oil - 30ml
- Honey - 15ml
- Salt - to taste
- Black pepper - to taste

**Instructions:**

1. To prepare your Tower Dual Basket Air Fryer for cooking, select the "Preheat" icon and allow it to warm up for approximately 3 minutes.
2. Toss the peeled and cubed butternut squash in a bowl with olive oil, ground cinnamon, ground cumin, coriander, honey, salt, and black pepper.
3. Place the seasoned butternut squash in the "left drawer" of the air fryer.
4. Press "Start/Pause" to roast them at 180°C using the "Vegetables" icon for 15 minutes.
5. Once the butternut squash is tender and caramelized, serve it as a flavourful and healthy side dish.

# Crispy Garlic Parmesan Green Beans

*Cooking Period: 15 mins / Serving Portions: 4*
*Per Serving: Calories 100, Carbs 8g, Fat 6g, Protein 4g*

**Ingredients:**

- Green beans - 400g, trimmed
- Grated Parmesan cheese - 30g
- Olive oil - 30ml
- Garlic - 2 cloves, minced
- Salt - to taste
- Black pepper - to taste

**Instructions:**

1. Preheat your Tower Dual Basket Air Fryer by pressing the "Preheat" icon and set the temperature to 180°C. Wait for 3 minutes until it's ready.
2. Toss the trimmed green beans with olive oil, minced garlic, salt, and black pepper in a bowl.
3. Place the seasoned green beans in the "left drawer" of the air fryer.
4. Press "Start/Pause" to cook them at 180°C using the "Vegetables" icon for 10 minutes.
5. Once the green beans are tender and slightly crispy, sprinkle them with grated Parmesan cheese and serve hot as a delightful and nutritious side dish.

# Fish and Seafood Recipes

# Grilled Lemon Herb Sea Bass

*Cooking Period: 20 mins / Serving Portions: 2*
*Per Serving: Calories 250, Carbs 5g, Fat 12g, Protein 30g*

**Ingredients:**

- Sea Bass Fillets - 2 (150g each)
- Lemon - 1, sliced
- Fresh Parsley - 5g, chopped
- Olive Oil - 20ml
- Salt - to taste
- Black Pepper - to taste
- Garlic - 2 cloves, minced

**Instructions:**

1. Start your Tower Dual Basket Air Fryer by selecting the "Preheat" icon; it requires 3 minutes to reach the desired temperature.
2. In the "left drawer" of the air fryer, lay out two large squares of aluminum foil.
3. Place the sea bass fillets in the center of each foil square.
4. Drizzle olive oil over the sea bass, sprinkle with chopped parsley, and season with salt, black pepper, and minced garlic.
5. Lay lemon slices on top of each fillet.
6. Fold the foil squares to create sealed parcels, ensuring no openings.
7. In the "right drawer" of the air fryer, place a sealed sea bass parcel.
8. Press "Match Cook" to cook them at the same time.
9. Cook both at 180°C using the "Fish" icon and adjust the time to 15 minutes.
10. Once the parcels are done, carefully open them and serve the sea bass hot.

# Crispy Garlic Prawns with Roasted Vegetables

*Cooking Period: 10 mins / Serving Portions: 2*
*Per Serving: Calories 280, Carbs 15g, Fat 14g, Protein 25g*

**Ingredients:**

- Large Prawns - 200g
- Bell Peppers - 150g, sliced
- Zucchini - 100g, sliced
- Red Onion - 100g, sliced
- Garlic - 3 cloves, minced
- Olive Oil - 25ml
- Paprika - 2g
- Salt - to taste
- Black Pepper - to taste
- Lemon Juice - 10ml

**Instructions:**

1. Begin preheating your Tower Dual Basket Air Fryer by pressing the "Preheat" button; it will be ready in 3 minutes.
2. In the "left drawer" of the air fryer, place the prawns.
3. In the "right drawer" of the air fryer, place the roasted vegetables (bell peppers, zucchini, and red onion).
4. Drizzle olive oil over the prawns and vegetables and then sprinkle with garlic, paprika, salt, and black pepper.
5. Use the "Smart Finish" function with the "Shrimp" icon for the prawns in the left drawer and set at 180°C for 8 minutes.
6. Use the "Vegetables" icon for the veggie mixture in the right drawer and set at 160°C for 10 minutes. Press "Start" to begin cooking.
7. Once done, drizzle lemon juice over the prawns and vegetables and serve hot.

# Tandoori-Style Salmon Tikka

*Cooking Period: 20 mins / Serving Portions: 2*
*Per Serving: Calories 280, Carbs 8g, Fat 14g, Protein 30g*

## Ingredients:

- Salmon Fillets - 2 (200g each)
- Greek Yogurt - 100g
- Tandoori Spice Mix - 10g
- Lime Juice - 10ml
- Fresh Cilantro - 5g, chopped
- Olive Oil - 20ml
- Salt - to taste
- Black Pepper - to taste

## Instructions:

1. Activate the preheat function on your Tower Dual Basket Air Fryer using the designated icon; wait 3 minutes until it's fully heated.
2. Combine Greek yogurt, tandoori spice mix, lime juice, chopped cilantro, olive oil, salt, and black pepper in a mixing bowl.
3. Coat the salmon fillets with the tandoori yogurt mixture.
4. In the "left drawer" of the air fryer, lay out two large squares of aluminum foil.
5. Place the marinated salmon fillets in the center of each foil square.
6. Cook at 180°C using the "Fish" icon for 15 minutes.
7. Once done, serve the Tandoori-Style Salmon Tikka hot with a side salad.

# Garlic Butter Shrimp and Herb-Roasted Asparagus

*Cooking Period: 20 mins / Serving Portions: 2*
*Per Serving: Calories 270, Carbs 10g, Fat 14g, Protein 25g*

## Ingredients:

- Large Shrimp - 200g
- Asparagus Spears - 200g
- Butter - 20g
- Fresh Thyme - 5g, chopped
- Lemon Zest - from 1 lemon
- Olive Oil - 20ml
- Garlic - 2 cloves, minced
- Salt - to taste
- Black Pepper - to taste

## Instructions:

1. To prepare your Tower Dual Basket Air Fryer, press the "Preheat" icon and wait 3 minutes for it to reach the optimal temperature.
2. Lay out one large square of aluminum foil into each drawer of the air fryer.
3. Place the shrimp in the center of each foil square.
4. Arrange asparagus spears around the shrimp, drizzle with olive oil, and season with salt, black pepper, and minced garlic.
5. Sprinkle chopped thyme and lemon zest over the shrimp and asparagus.
6. Place small pieces of butter on top.
7. Fold the foil squares to create sealed parcels, ensuring no openings.
8. Press "Match Cook" to cook them at the same time.
9. Cook both at 180°C using the "Shrimp" function for 8 minutes.
10. Once the parcels are done, carefully open them and serve the Garlic Butter Shrimp and Herb-Roasted Asparagus hot.

# Lemon-Dill Cod with Crispy Potato Wedges

*Cooking Period: 20 mins / Serving Portions: 2*
*Per Serving: Calories 280, Carbs 20g, Fat 12g, Protein 25g*

# Spicy Cajun Grilled Prawns with Avocado Salad

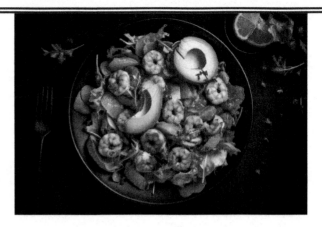

*Cooking Period: 20 mins / Serving Portions: 2*
*Per Serving: Calories 260, Carbs 10g, Fat 15g, Protein 25g*

## Ingredients:

- Cod Fillets - 2 (150g each)
- Potatoes - 200g, cut into wedges
- Lemon - 1, sliced
- Fresh Dill - 5g, chopped
- Olive Oil - 20ml
- Salt - to taste
- Black Pepper - to taste
- Garlic - 2 cloves, minced

## Instructions:

1. Set your Tower Dual Basket Air Fryer to preheat mode by pressing the corresponding icon; wait patiently for 3 minutes for it to be ready.
2. In the "left drawer" of the air fryer, lay out two large squares of aluminum foil.
3. Place the cod fillets in the center of each foil square.
4. Arrange potato wedges around the cod, and drizzle olive oil over the cod and potatoes.
5. Season with salt, black pepper, and minced garlic.
6. Lay lemon slices on each cod fillet and sprinkle with chopped dill.
7. Fold the foil squares to create sealed parcels, ensuring no openings.
8. In the "right drawer" of the air fryer, place a sealed cod and potato parcel.
9. Press "Match Cook" to cook them at the same time.
10. Cook both at 180°C using the "Fish" icon for 10 minutes. Cook for 5 more minutes if needed.
11. Once the parcels are done, carefully open them and serve the Lemon-Dill Cod with Crispy Potato Wedges hot.

## Ingredients:

- Large Prawns - 200g
- Avocado - 1, diced
- Cherry Tomatoes - 150g, halved
- Red Onion - 50g, thinly sliced
- Cajun Spice Mix - 10g
- Olive Oil - 20ml
- Lime Juice - 10ml
- Salt - to taste
- Black Pepper - to taste

## Instructions:

1. Initiate the preheating process on your Tower Dual Basket Air Fryer by pressing the "Preheat" option; it takes 3 minutes to heat up completely.
2. Place the prawns in the "left drawer" of the air fryer.
3. Drizzle olive oil over the prawns and sprinkle with Cajun spice mix, salt, and black pepper.
4. Cook at 180°C for 15 minutes using the "Shrimp" icon.
5. Combine diced avocado, halved cherry tomatoes, sliced red onion, and lime juice in a separate bowl. Toss to make the avocado salad.
6. Once done, serve the Spicy Cajun Grilled Prawns with Avocado Salad for a delicious and healthy meal.

# Baked Haddock with Mediterranean Quinoa Salad

# Cajun-Style Catfish with Roasted Corn and Peppers

*Cooking Period: 25 mins / Serving Portions: 2*
*Per Serving: Calories 290, Carbs 20g, Fat 15g, Protein 20g*

*Cooking Period: 10 mins / Serving Portions: 2*
*Per Serving: Calories 270, Carbs 20g, Fat 15g, Protein 20g*

## Ingredients:

- Haddock Fillets - 2 (150g each)
- Quinoa - 100g, cooked
- Cherry Tomatoes - 150g, halved
- Cucumber - 100g, diced
- Kalamata Olives - 20g, sliced
- Red Onion - 50g, finely chopped
- Fresh Parsley - 5g, chopped
- Olive Oil - 20ml
- Dijon Mustard - 10ml
- Lemon Juice - 10ml
- Fresh Basil - 5g, chopped
- Salt - to taste
- Black Pepper - to taste

## Instructions:

1. Preheat your Tower Dual Basket Air Fryer by pressing the "Preheat" icon and set the temperature to 180°C. Wait for 3 minutes until it's ready.
2. In the "left drawer" of the air fryer, lay out two large squares of aluminum foil.
3. Place the haddock fillets in the center of each foil square.
4. In the "right drawer," place quinoa, cherry tomatoes, cucumber, Kalamata olives, and red onion.
5. Press "Match Cook" to cook both drawers simultaneously.
6. Drizzle with olive oil and season with salt and black pepper.
7. In a small bowl, mix Dijon mustard and lemon juice. Brush the mixture over the haddock fillets.
8. Cook at 180°C using the "Fish" icon for 15 minutes.
9. After it's done, combine cooked quinoa, cherry tomatoes, cucumber, Kalamata olives, red onion, fresh parsley, and fresh basil in a mixing bowl. Drizzle with olive oil and season with salt and black pepper.
10. Once the parcels are done, carefully open them and serve the Bake Haddock with Mediterranean Quinoa Salad.

## Ingredients:

- Catfish Fillets - 2 (150g each)
- Corn Kernels - 150g
- Red Bell Pepper - 1 sliced
- Green Bell Pepper - 1, sliced
- Cajun Spice Mix - 10g
- Olive Oil - 20ml
- Salt - to taste
- Black Pepper - to taste
- Garlic - 2 cloves, minced

## Instructions:

1. Prepare your Tower Dual Basket Air Fryer by pressing the "Preheat" icon; it will take approximately 3 minutes to warm up.
2. In the "left drawer" of the air fryer, lay out two large squares of aluminum foil.
3. Place the catfish fillets in the center of each foil square.
4. Drizzle with olive oil and sprinkle with Cajun spice mix, salt, black pepper, and minced garlic.
5. In the "right drawer," place the corn kernels and sliced bell peppers. Drizzle with olive oil and season with salt and black pepper.
6. Use the "Smart Finish" function with the "Fish" icon for the pork in the left drawer and set at 180°C for 10 minutes.
7. Use the "Vegetables" icon for the bell pepper mixture in the right drawer and set at 160°C for 10 minutes. Press "Start" to begin cooking.
8. Once done, carefully open the foil parcels with catfish and serve with the roasted corn and peppers.

# Salmon with Green Beans & Tomatoes

*Cooking Period: 10 mins /Serving Portions: 4*
*Per Serving: Calories 310, Carbs 11.5g, Fat 14.6g, Protein 32.5g*

**Ingredients:**

- Fresh green beans - 455g, trimmed
- Cherry tomatoes - 225g
- Olive oil - 45ml, divided
- Salt, as required
- Garlic cloves - 2, minced
- Fresh dill - 5g, chopped
- Fresh lemon juice - 30ml
- Salmon fillets - 4 (140-g)

**Instructions:**

1. In a large bowl, add the green beans, tomatoes, 30ml of oil, and salt and toss to coat.
2. In a bowl, add the salmon fillets, remaining oil, garlic, dill, lemon juice, and salt and mix well.
3. Preheat your Tower Dual Basket Air Fryer using the "Pre-Heat" icon at 180°C and wait for 3 minutes.
4. In the "left drawer," place the salmon fillets.
5. In the "right drawer," place the green beans.
6. Use the "Smart Finish" function with the "Fish" icon for the salmon in the left drawer and set at 180°C for 10 minutes.
7. Use the "Vegetables" icon for the bell pepper mixture in the right drawer and set at 160°C for 10 minutes. Press "Start" to begin cooking.
8. After 5 minutes of cooking, flip the salmon fillets and green beans.
9. Once done, serve salmon hot alongside the green beans and tomatoes.

# Teriyaki Glazed Halibut with Sesame Broccoli

*Cooking Period: 15 mins /Serving Portions: 2*
*Per Serving: Calories 280, Carbs 15g, Fat 15g, Protein 25g*

**Ingredients:**

- Halibut Fillets - 2 (150g each)
- Broccoli Florets - 200g
- Teriyaki Sauce - 40ml
- Sesame Seeds - 10g
- Olive Oil - 20ml
- Salt - to taste
- Black Pepper - to taste
- Garlic - 2 cloves, minced

**Instructions:**

1. To prepare your Tower Dual Basket Air Fryer, initiate the "Preheat" mode, which will be ready in 3 minutes.
2. In the "left drawer" of the air fryer, lay out two large squares of aluminum foil.
3. Place the halibut fillets in the center of each foil square.
4. Drizzle with teriyaki sauce, and season with salt, black pepper, and minced garlic.
5. In the "right drawer," place the broccoli florets. Drizzle with olive oil and season with salt and black pepper.
6. Use the "Smart Finish" function with the "Fish" icon for the halibut in the left drawer and set at 180°C for 15 minutes.
7. Use the "Vegetables" icon for the broccoli in the right drawer and set at 160°C for 10 minutes. Press "Start" to begin cooking.
8. Once done, carefully open the foil parcels with halibut and transfer the broccoli onto a plate.
9. Sprinkle the broccoli with sesame seeds.
10. Serve the halibut with the sesame broccoli for a delightful and healthy meal.

# Poultry Recipes

# Balsamic Glazed Chicken Breasts with Roasted Vegetables

*Cooking Period: 25 mins* / *Serving Portions: 2*
*Per Serving: Calories 320, Carbs 15g, Fat 10g, Protein 35g*

# Herb-Crusted Turkey Cutlets with Mashed Potatoes

*Cooking Period: 30 mins* / *Serving Portions: 2*
*Per Serving: Calories 350, Carbs 20g, Fat 15g, Protein 30g*

## Balsamic Glazed Chicken Breasts with Roasted Vegetables

**Ingredients:**

- Chicken breasts - 2 (180g each)
- Red bell pepper - 150g, sliced
- Zucchini - 150g, sliced
- Red onion - 100g, sliced
- Balsamic vinegar - 30ml
- Olive oil - 20ml
- Dried oregano - 2g
- Salt - to taste
- Black pepper - to taste
- Garlic - 2 cloves, minced

**Instructions:**

1. Activate your Tower Dual Basket Air Fryer by selecting the "Preheat" icon. It will be ready in 3 minutes.
2. In the "left drawer," place the chicken breasts.
3. In the "right drawer," arrange the sliced red bell pepper, zucchini, and red onion.
4. Drizzle olive oil and balsamic vinegar over the chicken and vegetables.
5. Season with dried oregano, salt, black pepper, and minced garlic.
6. Use the "Smart Finish" icon to set different cooking times.
7. For the chicken, use the "Drumstick" icon with a time of 18 minutes and a temperature of 200°C.
8. Set the "Vegetables" icon for the vegetables to 180°C and adjust the time to 15 minutes.
9. Press "Start" to begin cooking.
10. Once done, serve the balsamic glazed chicken breasts alongside the roasted vegetables.

## Herb-Crusted Turkey Cutlets with Mashed Potatoes

**Ingredients:**

- Turkey cutlets - 2 (200g each)
- Potatoes - 300g, peeled and diced
- Fresh thyme - 5g, chopped
- Dijon mustard - 20ml
- Olive oil - 30ml
- Salt - to taste
- Black pepper - to taste
- Garlic - 2 cloves, minced

**Instructions:**

1. Preheat your Tower Dual Basket Air Fryer to 180°C using the "Preheat" icon and wait for 3 minutes.
2. In the "left drawer," place the turkey cutlets.
3. In the "right drawer," add the peeled and diced potatoes.
4. Drizzle olive oil over the turkey and potatoes.
5. Season the turkey with Dijon mustard, chopped fresh thyme, salt, black pepper, and minced garlic.
6. Use the "Smart Finish" icon to set different cooking times.
7. For the turkey, use the "Drumstick" icon with a time of 20 minutes and a temperature of 180°C.
8. Set the "French Fries" icon for 18 minutes for the potatoes at 200°C.
9. Press "Start" to begin cooking.
10. Once done, serve the herb-crusted turkey cutlets with mashed potatoes.

# Lemon-Herb Cornish Hens with Roasted Brussels Sprouts

# Crispy Skin Quail with Honey-Glazed Carrots

*Cooking Period: 35 mins / Serving Portions: 2*
*Per Serving: Calories 340, Carbs 12g, Fat 20g, Protein 30g*

*Cooking Period: 25 mins / Serving Portions: 2*
*Per Serving: Calories 330, Carbs 25g, Fat 12g, Protein 25g*

## Ingredients:

- Cornish hens - 2 (250g each)
- Brussels sprouts - 200g
- Lemon - 1, sliced
- Fresh rosemary - 5g, chopped
- Olive oil - 30ml
- Salt - to taste
- Black pepper - to taste
- Garlic - 2 cloves, minced

## Instructions:

1. Get your Tower Dual Basket Air Fryer ready for cooking by pressing the "Preheat" icon; it takes 3 minutes to warm up.
2. In the "left drawer," place the Cornish hens.
3. In the "right drawer," arrange the Brussels sprouts.
4. Drizzle olive oil over the Cornish hens and Brussels sprouts.
5. Season the Cornish hens with chopped fresh rosemary, salt, black pepper, and minced garlic.
6. Place lemon slices on top of each Cornish hen.
7. Use the "Smart Finish" icon to set different cooking times.
8. For the Cornish hens, set the time to 30 minutes and a temperature of 180°C.
9. For the Brussels sprouts, set the "Vegetables" icon to 160°C and the time to 20 minutes.
10. Press "Start" to begin cooking.
11. Once done, serve the lemon-herb Cornish hens with roasted Brussels sprouts. Enjoy a delightful feast.

## Ingredients:

- Quail - 4 (100g each)
- Carrots - 200g, sliced into sticks
- Honey - 30ml
- Olive oil - 20ml
- Fresh thyme - 5g, chopped
- Salt - to taste
- Black pepper - to taste
- Garlic - 2 cloves, minced

## Instructions:

1. Set your Tower Dual Basket Air Fryer to preheat mode by pressing the "Preheat" icon; reaching the desired temperature will take 3 minutes.
2. In the "left drawer," place the quail.
3. In the "right drawer," arrange the sliced carrots.
4. Drizzle olive oil over the quail and carrots.
5. Season the quail with honey, chopped fresh thyme, salt, black pepper, and minced garlic.
6. For the quail, manually set the temperature at 180°C for 30 minutes.
7. For the carrots, set the "Vegetables" at 160°C and adjust the time to 20 minutes.
8. Press "Start" to begin cooking.
9. Once done, serve the crispy skin quail alongside honey-glazed carrots.

# Spiced Chicken Drumsticks with Sweet Potato Wedges

*Cooking Period: 30 mins / Serving Portions: 2*
*Per Serving: Calories 320, Carbs 30g, Fat 15g, Protein 25g*

**Ingredients:**

- Chicken drumsticks - 4 (200g total)
- Sweet potatoes - 300g, cut into wedges
- Paprika - 5g
- Cumin - 5g
- Olive oil - 30ml
- Salt - to taste
- Black pepper - to taste
- Garlic - 2 cloves, minced

**Instructions:**

1. Preheat your Tower Dual Basket Air Fryer to 200°C using the "Preheat" icon and wait for 3 minutes.
2. In the "left drawer," place the chicken drumsticks.
3. In the "right drawer," arrange the sweet potato wedges.
4. Drizzle olive oil over the drumsticks and sweet potatoes.
5. Season the chicken with paprika, cumin, salt, black pepper, and minced garlic.
6. Use the "Smart Finish" icon to set different cooking times.
7. For the chicken drumsticks, use the "Drumsticks" icon with a time of 20 minutes and a temperature of 200°C.
8. Set the "French Fries" icon for the sweet potatoes for 18 minutes at 200°C.
9. Press "Start" to begin cooking.
10. Once done, serve the spiced chicken drumsticks with sweet potato wedges. Enjoy a flavourful dinner.

# Rosemary Roasted Turkey Thighs with Cranberry Sauce

*Cooking Period: 30 mins / Serving Portions: 2*
*Per Serving: Calories 330, Carbs 25g, Fat 15g, Protein 30g*

**Ingredients:**

- Turkey thighs - 2 (250g each)
- Cranberries - 100g
- Fresh rosemary - 5g, chopped
- Olive oil - 30ml
- Salt - to taste
- Black pepper - to taste
- Garlic - 2 cloves, minced

**Instructions:**

1. Preheat your Tower Dual Basket Air Fryer to 180°C using the "Preheat" icon and wait for 3 minutes.
2. In the "left drawer," place the turkey thighs.
3. In the "right drawer," add the cranberries.
4. Drizzle olive oil over the turkey thighs and cranberries.
5. Season the turkey with chopped fresh rosemary, salt, black pepper, and minced garlic.
6. For the turkey, manually set the temperature at 180°C for 30 minutes.
7. Set the "Vegetable" icon for the cranberries for 10 minutes at 160°C.
8. Press "Start" to begin cooking.
9. Once done, serve the rosemary-roasted turkey thighs with cranberry sauce. Enjoy a festive meal.

# Spiced Turkey Meatballs with Mediterranean Quinoa Salad

# Spicy Buffalo Chicken Wings with Blue Cheese Dip

*Cooking Period: 30 mins / Serving Portions: 2*
*Per Serving: Calories 320, Carbs 25g, Fat 12g, Protein 25g*

*Cooking Period: 30 mins / Serving Portions: 2*
*Per Serving: Calories 340, Carbs 5g, Fat 20g, Protein 30g*

## Ingredients:

- Turkey meatballs - 250g
- Quinoa - 150g, cooked
- Cherry tomatoes - 150g, halved
- Cucumber - 100g, diced
- Red onion - 50g, finely chopped
- Ground cumin - 2g
- Olive oil - 20ml
- Salt - to taste
- Black pepper - to taste
- Lemon juice - 20ml

## Instructions:

1. Press the "Preheat" icon to let your Tower Dual Basket Air Fryer heat at 180°C for 3 minutes.
2. In the "left drawer," place the turkey meatballs.
3. In the "right drawer," add the cooked quinoa, cherry tomatoes, cucumber, and red onion.
4. Drizzle olive oil over the turkey meatballs and the quinoa salad.
5. Season the turkey meatballs with ground cumin, salt, black pepper, and minced garlic.
6. Use the "Smart Finish" icon to set different cooking times.
7. For the turkey meatballs, manually set the temperature at 180°C for 20 minutes.
8. For the quinoa salad, use the "Vegetable" icon at 160°C for 10 minutes.
9. Press "Start" to begin cooking the turkey meatballs.
10. Once done, mix the turkey meatballs with the quinoa salad and drizzle lemon juice over the salad. Enjoy a Mediterranean-inspired dish.

## Ingredients:

- Chicken wings - 300g
- Hot sauce - 30ml
- Butter - 30g, melted
- Paprika - 2g
- Olive oil - 20ml
- Salt - to taste
- Black pepper - to taste
- Blue cheese dressing - for dipping

## Instructions:

1. First, Preheat your Tower Dual Basket Air Fryer to 200°C using the "Preheat" icon and wait for 3 minutes.
2. In the "left drawer," place the chicken wings.
3. Mix hot sauce, melted butter, paprika, olive oil, salt, and black pepper in a bowl.
4. Brush the hot sauce mixture over the chicken wings.
5. Set the time for 20 minutes at 200°C.
6. Press "Start" to begin cooking.
7. Once done, serve the spicy buffalo chicken wings with a blue cheese dip.

# Mango Salsa Chicken Breast

*Cooking Period: 30 mins / Serving Portions: 2*
*Per Serving: Calories 320, Carbs 20g, Fat 12g, Protein 30g*

**Ingredients:**

- Chicken breasts - 2 (180g each)
- Ripe mango - 1, diced
- Red bell pepper - 100g, diced
- Red onion - 50g, finely chopped
- Fresh cilantro - 5g, chopped
- Lime juice - 30ml
- Olive oil - 20ml
- Salt - to taste
- Black pepper - to taste
- Garlic - 2 cloves, minced

**Instructions:**

1. Preheat your Tower Dual Basket Air Fryer to 180°C using the "Preheat" icon and wait for 3 minutes.
2. In the "left drawer," place the chicken breasts.
3. Mix diced mango, diced red bell pepper, finely chopped red onion, chopped fresh cilantro, lime juice, olive oil, salt, black pepper, and minced garlic to create the mango salsa.
4. Spoon the mango salsa over the chicken breasts.
5. Set the same time for 20 minutes at 180°C.
6. Press "Start" to begin cooking.
7. Once done, serve the mango salsa chicken breast with a generous spoonful of the fresh mango salsa on top.

# Soy-Ginger Glazed Chicken Thighs

*Cooking Period: 30 mins / Serving Portions: 2*
*Per Serving: Calories 340, Carbs 15g, Fat 20g, Protein 30g*

**Ingredients:**

- Chicken thighs - 2 (200g each)
- Soy sauce - 30ml
- Honey - 30ml
- Fresh ginger - 5g, minced
- Garlic - 2 cloves, minced
- Olive oil - 20ml
- Sesame seeds - 2g
- Green onions - 2, sliced
- Salt - to taste
- Black pepper - to taste

**Instructions:**

1. Heat your Tower Dual Basket Air Fryer to 180°C using the "Preheat" icon and wait for some time.
2. In the "left drawer," place the chicken thighs.
3. In a bowl, mix soy sauce, honey, minced fresh ginger, minced garlic, olive oil, sesame seeds, salt, and black pepper to create the soy-ginger glaze.
4. Brush the soy-ginger glaze over the chicken thighs.
5. Manually set the temperature at 180°C for 15 minutes.
6. Press "Start" to begin cooking.
7. Once done, serve the soy-ginger glazed chicken thighs garnished with sliced green onions.

# Buffalo Chicken Tenders

*Cooking Period: 20 mins /Serving Portions: 2*
*Per Serving: Calories 320, Carbs 5g, Fat 15g, Protein 35g*

**Ingredients:**

- Chicken tenders - 250g
- Hot sauce - 30ml
- Butter - 30g, melted
- Paprika - 2g
- Olive oil - 20ml
- Salt - to taste
- Black pepper - to taste
- Blue cheese dressing - for dipping

**Instructions:**

1. Preheat your Tower Dual Basket Air Fryer to 200°C using the "Preheat" icon and wait for 3 minutes.
2. In the "left drawer," place the chicken tenders.
3. Mix hot sauce, melted butter, paprika, olive oil, salt, and black pepper in a bowl to create the buffalo sauce.
4. Brush the buffalo sauce over the chicken tenders.
5. Set the time for 18 minutes at 180°C using the icon "Drumsticks."
6. Press "Start" to begin cooking.
7. Once done, serve the buffalo chicken tenders with a blue cheese dressing.

# Lemon Garlic Roasted Duck Legs

*Cooking Period: 30 mins /Serving Portions: 2*
*Per Serving: Calories 380, Carbs 10g, Fat 25g, Protein 35g*

**Ingredients:**

- Duck legs - 2 (about 250g each)
- Lemon - 1, sliced
- Fresh thyme - 5g, chopped
- Olive oil - 30ml
- Salt - to taste
- Black pepper - to taste
- Garlic - 3 cloves, minced

**Instructions:**

1. Preheat your Tower Dual Basket Air Fryer to 180°C using the "Preheat" icon and wait for 3 minutes.
2. In the "left drawer," place the duck legs.
3. Drizzle olive oil over the duck legs.
4. Season the duck legs with chopped fresh thyme, salt, black pepper, and minced garlic.
5. Place lemon slices on top of each duck leg.
6. For the duck legs, use the "Drumstick" icon with a time of 22 minutes and a temperature of 180°C. Cook for 10 more minutes if needed.
7. Press "Start" to begin cooking.
8. Once done, serve the lemon garlic roasted duck legs. A succulent and flavourful dinner.

# Turkey and Cranberry Stuffed Peppers

*Cooking Period: 23 mins / Serving Portions: 4*
*Per Serving: Calories 350, Carbs 40g, Fat 10g, Protein 25g*

# Spicy Peri-Peri Chicken Thighs with Coconut Rice

*Cooking Period: 30 mins / Serving Portions: 4*
*Per Serving: Calories 400, Carbs 30g, Fat 20g, Protein 25g*

## Ingredients:

- Bell peppers - 4, tops removed and seeds discarded
- Ground turkey - 400g
- Cranberries - 50g, dried
- Onion - 1, finely chopped
- Garlic - 2 cloves, minced
- Olive oil - 30ml
- Salt - to taste
- Black pepper - to taste
- Fresh parsley - 5g, chopped

## Instructions:

1. Preheat your Tower Dual Basket Air Fryer using the "Preheat" icon. It will take 3 minutes.
2. In a skillet, heat the olive oil over medium heat. Add the chopped onion and minced garlic. Sauté until the onion becomes translucent.
3. Add the ground turkey and cook until browned. Season with salt and black pepper.
4. In a bowl, combine the dried cranberries and chopped fresh parsley. Mix in the cooked turkey and onion mixture.
5. Stuff each bell pepper with the turkey and cranberry mixture.
6. Place the stuffed peppers in the "left drawer" of the air fryer and use the "Vegetables" icon for 160°C.
7. Press "Start" to begin cooking. Wait for 20 minutes till it's completely cooked.
8. Once done, serve the turkey and cranberry stuffed peppers.

## Ingredients:

- Chicken thighs - 8
- Peri-Peri sauce - 60ml
- Basmati rice - 1 cup, uncooked
- Coconut milk - 400ml
- Red bell pepper - 1, diced
- Onion - 1, finely chopped
- Garlic - 3 cloves, minced
- Olive oil - 30ml
- Salt - to taste
- Black pepper - to taste
- Fresh cilantro - 5g, chopped

## Instructions:

1. Preheat your Tower Dual Basket Air Fryer using the "Pre-Heat" icon until ready.
2. In the "left drawer," place the chicken thighs.
3. Mix the Peri-Peri sauce, olive oil, minced garlic, salt, and black pepper in a bowl.
4. Brush the chicken thighs with the Peri-Peri mixture.
5. In the "right drawer," place a tray with uncooked basmati rice, diced red bell pepper, finely chopped onion, and coconut milk.
6. Use the "Smart Finish" icon to set different cooking times.
7. For the chicken thighs, use the "Drumsticks" icon for 20 minutes at 200°C.
8. For the rice and coconut mixture, use the "Vegetables" icon for 30 minutes at 180°C.
9. Press "Start" to begin cooking.
10. Once done, serve the spicy Peri-Peri chicken thighs with coconut rice garnished with fresh cilantro.

# Turkey Meatballs with Zucchini Noodles

*Cooking Period: 30 mins / Serving Portions: 4*
*Per Serving: Calories 320, Carbs 15g, Fat 15g, Protein 30g*

# Lemon Pepper Chicken with Mediterranean Rice

*Cooking Period: 35 mins / Serving Portions: 4*
*Per Serving: Calories 380, Carbs 30g, Fat 15g, Protein 30g*

**Ingredients:**

- Ground turkey - 500g
- Zucchini - 2, spiralized into noodles
- Onion - 1, finely chopped
- Garlic - 3 cloves, minced
- Olive oil - 30ml
- Tomato sauce - 500ml
- Parmesan cheese - 50g, grated
- Salt - to taste
- Black pepper - to taste
- Fresh basil - 10g, chopped

**Instructions:**

1. Preheat your Tower Dual Basket Air Fryer using the "Pre-Heat" icon at 180°C.
2. Combine the ground turkey, minced garlic, chopped onion, salt, and black pepper in a bowl. Form the mixture into meatballs.
3. In the "left drawer," place the turkey meatballs.
4. Place the spiralized zucchini noodles in the "right drawer" and drizzle with olive oil, salt, and black pepper.
5. Use the "Match Cook" icon to set the same time and temperature for both drawers. Set the time for 20 minutes at 180°C.
6. Press "Start" to begin cooking.
7. In the last 5 minutes, add the tomato sauce to the zucchini noodles in the "right drawer."
8. Once done, serve the turkey meatballs with zucchini noodles, garnished with grated Parmesan cheese and chopped fresh basil.

**Ingredients:**

- Chicken breasts - 4
- Lemon zest - from 2 lemons
- Lemon juice - 60ml
- Olive oil - 30ml
- Garlic - 3 cloves, minced
- Salt - to taste
- Black pepper - to taste
- Basmati rice - 1 cup, uncooked
- Mixed Mediterranean vegetables - 300g
- Fresh oregano - 10g, chopped

**Instructions:**

1. Preheat your Tower Dual Basket Air Fryer using the "Pre-Heat" icon at 180°C.
2. In the "left drawer," place the chicken breasts.
3. Mix lemon zest, lemon juice, olive oil, minced garlic, salt, and black pepper in a bowl.
4. Brush the chicken breasts with the lemon mixture.
5. In the "right drawer," place a tray with uncooked basmati rice, mixed Mediterranean vegetables, and chopped fresh oregano.
6. Use the "Smart Finish" icon to set different cooking times.
7. Use the "Drumsticks" icon for the chicken breasts for 20 minutes at 200°C.
8. For the rice and vegetable mixture, use the "Vegetables" icon for 25 minutes at 180°C.
9. Press "Start" to begin cooking.
10. Once done, serve the lemon pepper chicken with Mediterranean rice.

# Chicken and Leek Pie with Creamy Mashed Potato

*Cooking Period: 30 mins / Serving Portions: 4*
*Per Serving: Calories 400, Carbs 30g, Fat 20g, Protein 25g*

## Ingredients:

- Chicken breast - 400g, diced
- Leeks - 2, sliced
- Butter - 30g
- Flour - 30g
- Chicken broth - 500ml
- Cream - 100ml
- Mashed potatoes - 500g
- Salt - to taste
- Black pepper - to taste
- Fresh thyme - 5g, chopped

## Instructions:

1. Begin by Preheating your Tower Dual Basket Air Fryer using the "Pre-Heat" icon for 3 minutes.
2. In the "left drawer," place the diced chicken breast.
3. Melt the butter and sauté the sliced leeks in a skillet until tender.
4. Sprinkle the flour over the leeks and stir well to create a roux.
5. Gradually add the chicken broth and cream, stirring continuously to create a creamy sauce. Season with salt, black pepper, and chopped fresh thyme.
6. Pour the leek and chicken mixture into a pie dish.
7. In the "right drawer," place a tray of creamy mashed potatoes.
8. Manually set the temperature for the chicken in the left drawer at 180°C for 30 minutes.
9. Use the "Vegetables" icon for the mashed potatoes in the right drawer, both for 25 minutes.
10. Press "Start" to begin cooking.
11. Once done, serve the Chicken and Leek Pie with Creamy Mashed Potato.

# Spicy Szechuan Duck with Vegetable Fried Rice

*Cooking Period: 40 mins / Serving Portions: 4*
*Per Serving: Calories 420, Carbs 40g, Fat 20g, Protein 25g*

## Ingredients:

- Duck breast - 2
- Szechuan sauce - 60ml
- Cooked rice - 2 cups
- Mixed vegetables - 200g
- Garlic - 3 cloves, minced
- Olive oil - 30ml
- Salt - to taste
- Black pepper - to taste
- Fresh cilantro - 5g, chopped

## Instructions:

1. Preheat your Tower Dual Basket Air Fryer; this is necessary to ensure the best-cooked meal. Use the "Preheat" icon at 180°C.
2. In the "left drawer," place the duck breasts.
3. Mix the Szechuan sauce, minced garlic, salt, and black pepper in a bowl.
4. Brush the duck breasts with the Szechuan sauce mixture.
5. In the "right drawer," place a tray of cooked rice and mixed vegetables. Drizzle with olive oil, salt, and black pepper.
6. Manually set the temperature for the duck in the left drawer at 180°C for 30 minutes.
7. Use the "Vegetables" icon for the rice and vegetables in the right drawer, both set at 160°C for 10 minutes.
8. Press "Start" to begin cooking.
9. Once done, serve the Spicy Szechuan Duck with Vegetable Fried Rice, garnished with fresh cilantro.

# Chicken Thighs with Carrots

*Cooking Period: 15 mins / Serving Portions: 4*
*Per Serving: Calories 339, Carbs 4.4g, Fat 20.3g, Protein 33.4g*

**Ingredients:**

- Chicken thighs - 4 (140-g)
- Olive oil - 45ml, divided
- Fresh lemon juice - 30ml
- fresh rosemary - 5g, chopped
- Salt and ground black pepper - to taste
- Carrots - 3, peeled and sliced

**Instructions:**

1. In a large bowl, add chicken thighs, 30ml of oil, lemon juice, rosemary, salt and pepper and mix well.
2. In another bowl, add carrot slices, remaining oil, salt and black pepper and toss to coat.
3. Preheat your Tower Dual Basket Air Fryer using the "Pre-Heat" icon at 180°C and wait for 3 minutes.
4. In the "left drawer," place the chicken thighs.
5. In the "right drawer," place the carrot slices.
6. Use the "Smart Finish" function with the "Drumstick" icon for the chicken thighs in the left drawer and set at 180°C for 15 minutes.
7. Use the "Vegetables" icon for the carrots in the right drawer and set at 160°C for 10 minutes. Press "Start" to begin cooking.
8. Once done, serve the chicken thighs with carrots.

# Sweet & Spicy Chicken Drumsticks with Potato Wedges

*Cooking Period: 20 mins / Serving Portions: 4*
*Per Serving: Calories 469, Carbs 27.4g, Fat 26.1g, Protein 30.2g*

**Ingredients:**

- Vegetable oil - 60ml, divided
- Garlic clove - 1, crushed
- Brown sugar - 10g
- Ground cumin - 5g
- Cayenne pepper - 5g
- Red chili powder - 2g
- Salt and ground black pepper - as required
- Chicken drumsticks - 4
- Large potatoes - 3, scrubbed and cut into wedges

**Instructions:**

1. In a large bowl, mix together 30ml of oil, garlic, brown sugar, spices, salt and black pepper.
2. Add the chicken drumsticks and coat with marinade generously.
3. Refrigerate to marinate for about 20-30 minutes.
4. In another bowl, add potato wedges, remaining oil, salt and black pepper and toss to coat well.
5. In the "left drawer," place the chicken drumsticks.
6. In the "right drawer," place the potato wedges.
7. Use the "Smart Finish" function with the "Drumstick" icon for the chicken drumsticks in the left drawer and set at 200°C for 20 minutes.
8. Use the "Vegetables" icon for the potato wedges in the right drawer and set at 160°C for 10 minutes. Press "Start" to begin cooking.
9. Once done, serve the chicken drumsticks with potato wedges.

# Meat Recipes

# Lamb Koftas with Flatbread || Lamb Chops with Vegetables

*Cooking Period: 30 mins / Serving Portions: 4*
*Per Serving: Calories 400, Carbs 30g, Fat 20g, Protein 25g*

*Cooking Period: 25 mins / Serving Portions: 2*
*Per Serving: Calories 400, Carbs 15g, Fat 20g, Protein 30g*

## Ingredients:

- Ground lamb - 500g
- Red onion - 1, finely chopped
- Fresh mint - 10g, chopped
- Ground cumin - 2g
- Ground coriander - 2g
- Paprika - 2g
- Olive oil - 30ml
- Salt - to taste
- Black pepper - to taste
- Wooden skewers soaked in water
- Flatbreads - 4

## Instructions:

1. Preheat your Tower Dual Basket Air Fryer using the "Pre-Heat" icon at 180°C and wait for 3 minutes.
2. In the "left drawer," place the ground lamb, and in the "right drawer," place flatbreads to warm them up.
3. Combine the chopped red onion, fresh mint, ground cumin, coriander, paprika, olive oil, salt, and black pepper with the ground lamb in a bowl.
4. Divide the mixture into equal portions and shape them into sausage-like koftas. Thread the koftas onto the soaked wooden skewers.
5. Use the "Smart Finish" icon with the " Steak" icon for the lamb koftas in the left drawer and the "Pizza" icon for warming the flatbreads in the right drawer, both set at 180°C for 15 minutes.
6. Press "Start" to begin cooking.
7. Once done, serve the lamb koftas with warm flatbreads.

## Ingredients:

- Lamb chops - 4
- Olive oil - 30ml
- Rosemary - 5g, chopped
- Garlic - 3 cloves, minced
- Salt - to taste
- Black pepper - to taste
- Mixed vegetables - 300g

## Instructions:

1. Preheat your Tower Dual Basket Air Fryer using the "Pre-Heat" icon at 180°C and wait for 3 minutes.
2. In the "left drawer," place the lamb chops; in the "right drawer," place a tray of mixed vegetables.
3. Mix the olive oil, chopped rosemary, minced garlic, salt, and black pepper in a bowl.
4. Brush the lamb chops with the olive oil and herb mixture, coating them evenly.
5. Use the "Smart Finish" icon with the "Steak" icon for the lamb chops in the left drawer and set at 180°C for 14 minutes. Use the "Vegetables" icon for the mixed vegetables in the right drawer and set at 180°C for 20 minutes.
6. Press "Start" to begin cooking.
7. Once done, serve the lamb chops with the mixed vegetables.

# Greek-Style Lamb Souvlaki Skewers

*Cooking Period: 25 mins / Serving Portions: 4*
*Per Serving: Calories 400, Carbs 20g, Fat 20g, Protein 30g*

## Ingredients:

- Lamb shoulder or leg meat - 500g, cubed
- Greek yogurt - 150ml
- Lemon juice - 30ml
- Olive oil - 30ml
- Garlic - 4 cloves, minced
- Oregano - 10g, dried
- Salt - to taste
- Black pepper - to taste
- Red onion - 1, cut into chunks
- Bell peppers - 2, cut into chunks
- Cherry tomatoes - 8
- Wooden skewers - 8, soaked in water

## Instructions:

1. Preheat your Tower Dual Basket Air Fryer using the "Pre-Heat" icon at 180°C and wait for 3 minutes.
2. Mix the Greek yogurt, lemon juice, olive oil, minced garlic, dried oregano, salt, and black pepper in a bowl to create the marinade.
3. Thread the cubed lamb, red onion, bell peppers, and cherry tomatoes onto the soaked wooden skewers.
4. Place the lamb skewers in the "left drawer" of the air fryer.
5. Brush the skewers with the yogurt marinade.
6. Set the time to 15 minutes at 200°C using the "Steak" icon.
7. Press "Start" to begin cooking.
8. Once done, serve the Greek-style lamb Souvlaki Skewers with pita bread and tzatziki.

# Lamb and Chickpea Stew

*Cooking Period: 1 hour / Serving Portions: 4*
*Per Serving: Calories 350, Carbs 20g, Fat 15g, Protein 30g*

## Ingredients:

- Lamb stew meat - 500g, cubed
- Onion - 1, chopped
- Garlic - 4 cloves, minced
- Chickpeas - 400g, cooked
- Canned tomatoes - 400g, crushed
- Lamb or vegetable broth - 500ml
- Olive oil - 30ml
- Cumin - 10g, ground
- Paprika - 10g, smoked
- Salt - to taste
- Black pepper - to taste
- Fresh parsley - 5g, chopped

## Instructions:

1. Preheat your Tower Dual Basket Air Fryer using the "Pre-Heat" icon at 180°C and wait for 3 minutes.
2. In the "left drawer," place the cubed lamb stew meat.
3. In a skillet, heat the olive oil over medium heat. Add the chopped onion and minced garlic. Sauté until the onion is soft.
4. Add the ground cumin and smoked paprika and stir for a minute.
5. Add the crushed canned tomatoes, cooked chickpeas, and lamb or vegetable broth. Season with salt and black pepper.
6. Pour the tomato-chickpea mixture over the lamb in the "left drawer."
7. Manually set the temperature at 180°C for 40 minutes for the lamb in the left drawer.
8. Press "Start" to begin cooking.
9. Once done, serve the Lamb and Chickpea Stew, garnished with fresh parsley. It's a hearty and warming dish.

# Lamb and Spinach Curry

# Lemon Herb Marinated Lamb Steaks

*Cooking Period: 30 mins / Serving Portions: 4*
*Per Serving: Calories 380, Carbs 25g, Fat 20g, Protein 30g*

*Cooking Period: 20 mins / Serving Portions: 2*
*Per Serving: Calories 400, Carbs 5g, Fat 20g, Protein 30g*

## Ingredients:

- Lamb shoulder or leg meat - 500g, cubed
- Onion - 1, chopped
- Garlic - 4 cloves, minced
- Spinach - 200g, chopped
- Canned tomatoes - 400g, crushed
- Lamb or vegetable broth - 500ml
- Olive oil - 30ml
- Curry powder - 15g
- Cumin - 10g, ground
- Garam masala - 10g
- Salt - to taste
- Black pepper - to taste
- Fresh cilantro - 5g, chopped

## Instructions:

1. Preheat your Tower Dual Basket Air Fryer using the "Pre-Heat" icon at 180°C and wait for 3 minutes.
2. In the "left drawer," place the cubed lamb.
3. In a skillet, heat the olive oil over medium heat. Add the chopped onion and minced garlic. Sauté until the onion is soft.
4. Add the curry powder, ground cumin, and garam masala, and stir for a minute.
5. Add the crushed canned tomatoes, lamb or vegetable broth, and chopped spinach. Season with salt and black pepper.
6. Pour the spinach-lamb mixture over the lamb in the "left drawer."
7. Set at 180°C for 25 minutes.
8. Press "Start" to begin cooking.
9. Once done, serve the Lamb and Spinach Curry, garnished with fresh cilantro.

## Ingredients:

- Lamb steaks - 2 (about 200g each)
- Lemon zest - from 1 lemon
- Fresh rosemary - 5g, chopped
- Garlic - 2 cloves, minced
- Olive oil - 30ml
- Salt - to taste
- Black pepper - to taste

## Instructions:

1. Preheat your Tower Dual Basket Air Fryer using the "Pre-Heat" icon.
2. Mix the lemon zest, chopped rosemary, minced garlic, olive oil, salt, and black pepper in a bowl to create the marinade.
3. Place the lamb steaks in the marinade and coat them thoroughly.
4. In the "left drawer," place the marinated lamb steaks.
5. Manually set the time and temperature for the drawer, 15 minutes at 200°C.
6. Press "Start" to begin cooking.
7. Once done, serve the Lemon Herb Marinated Lamb Steaks with your choice of sides.

# Lamb Steak and Broccoli Bake

*Cooking Period: 14 mins* / *Serving Portions: 4*
*Per Serving: Calories 356, Carbs 8g, Fat 12.9g, Protein 50.1g*

**Ingredients:**

- Onion - ½, roughly chopped
- Garlic cloves - 5, peeled
- Fresh ginger - 5g, peeled
- Ground cumin - 5g
- Cayenne pepper - 5g
- Salt and ground black pepper - to taste
- Boneless lamb steaks - 1½ pounds
- Broccoli - 1 head, cut into florets

**Instructions:**

1. In a blender, add the onion, garlic, ginger, and spices and pulse until smooth.
2. Transfer the mixture into a large bowl.
3. Add the lamb steaks and generously coat with the mixture.
4. Refrigerate to marinate for about 24 hours.
5. First, you'll have to preheat your Tower Dual Basket Air Fryer using the "Pre-Heat" icon and wait for 3 minutes.
6. In the "left drawer," place the lamb steaks.
7. In the "right drawer," place the broccoli florets.
8. Use the "Smart Finish" icon with the "Steak" icon for the lamb in the left drawer and set at 180°C for 14 minutes.
9. Use the "Vegetables" icon for the broccoli in the right drawer and set at 160°C for 10 minutes. Press "Start" to begin cooking.
10. Once done, serve the Lamb and Broccoli Bake.

# Rack of Lamb with Green Beans

*Cooking Period: 14 mins* / *Serving Portions: 5*
*Per Serving: Calories 280, Carbs 6.9g, Fat 15g, Protein 29.2g*

**Ingredients:**

- Butter - 20g, melted
- Garlic clove - 1, finely chopped
- Rack of lamb - 1¾lb.
- Salt and ground black pepper - to taste
- Egg - 1
- Panko breadcrumbs - 75g
- Fresh thyme - 5g, minced
- Fresh rosemary - 5g, minced
- Green beans - 680g, trimmed and sliced
- Olive oil - 30ml

**Instructions:**

1. In a bowl, mix together the butter, garlic, salt, and black pepper.
2. Coat the rack of lamb with garlic mixture.
3. In a shallow dish, beat the egg.
4. In another dish, mix together the breadcrumbs and herbs.
5. Dip the rack of lamb in beaten egg and then, coat with breadcrumbs mixture.
6. In a bowl, add green beans, oil, salt and pepper and toss to coat.
7. Preheat your Tower Dual Basket Air Fryer using the "Pre-Heat" icon for 3 minutes.
8. In the "left drawer," place the rack of lamb.
9. Place the green bean in the "right drawer."
10. Use the "Smart Finish" icon with the "Steak" icon for the lamb in the left drawer and set at 180°C for 14 minutes.
11. Use the "Vegetables" icon for the green beans in the right drawer and set at 160°C for 10 minutes. Press "Start" to begin cooking.
12. Once done, place the rack of lamb onto a cutting board for about 5 minutes
13. Cut the rack of lamb into individual chops and serve alongside the green beans.

# Lamb Meatballs and Rice

*Cooking Period: 25 mins / Serving Portions: 4*
*Per Serving: Calories 380, Carbs 30g, Fat 20g, Protein 20g*

**Ingredients:**

- Ground lamb - 500g
- Rice - 2 cups
- Onion - 1, chopped
- Garlic - 3 cloves, minced
- Cumin - 10g, ground
- Cilantro - 10g, chopped
- Olive oil - 30ml
- Salt - to taste
- Black pepper - to taste

**Instructions:**

1. Preheat your Tower Dual Basket Air Fryer using the "Pre-Heat" icon at 180°C and wait for 3 minutes.
2. Mix the ground lamb, chopped onion, minced garlic, ground cumin, chopped cilantro, salt, and black pepper to form meatballs in a bowl.
3. In the "left drawer," place the lamb meatballs.
4. In the "right drawer," place the rice pot with water.
5. Use the "Match Cook" icon to set the same time and temperature for both drawers, 20 minutes at 180°C.
6. Press "Start" to begin cooking.
7. Once done, serve the Lamb Meatballs and Rice.

# Beef and Mushroom Pie

*Cooking Period: 45 mins / Serving Portions: 4*
*Per Serving: Calories 400, Carbs 20g, Fat 20g, Protein 30g*

**Ingredients:**

- Beef stew meat - 500g, cubed
- Mushrooms - 200g, sliced
- Onion - 1, chopped
- Garlic - 3 cloves, minced
- Puff pastry - 1 sheet
- Beef or vegetable broth - 500ml
- Olive oil - 30ml
- Worcestershire sauce - 30ml
- Thyme - 10g, dried
- Salt - to taste
- Black pepper - to taste

**Instructions:**

1. Preheat your Tower Dual Basket Air Fryer using the "Pre-Heat" before cooking.
2. In the "left drawer," place the cubed beef stew meat.
3. In a skillet, heat the olive oil over medium heat. Add the chopped onion and minced garlic. Sauté until the onion is soft.
4. Add the sliced mushrooms and dried thyme and stir for a few minutes.
5. Add the beef or vegetable broth and Worcestershire sauce. Season with salt and black pepper.
6. Pour the mushroom and beef mixture into a pie dish.
7. Roll out the puff pastry and place it on the pie dish, sealing the edges.
8. Manually set the temperature and time at 180°C for 40 minutes.
9. Press "Start" to begin cooking.
10. Once done, serve the Beef and Mushroom Pie.

# Beef and Bean Chili

*Cooking Period: 35 mins /Serving Portions: 6*
*Per Serving: Calories 350, Carbs 25g, Fat 15g, Protein 25g*

## Ingredients:

- Ground beef - 500g
- Red kidney beans - 400g, canned and drained
- Onion - 1, chopped
- Garlic - 3 cloves, minced
- Bell peppers - 2, diced
- Canned tomatoes - 400g, crushed
- Chili powder - 15g
- Cumin - 10g, ground
- Paprika - 10g
- Salt - to taste
- Black pepper - to taste
- Olive oil - 30ml

## Instructions:

1. Preheat your Tower Dual Basket Air Fryer using the "Pre-Heat" icon at 180°C and wait for 3 minutes.
2. In a skillet, heat the olive oil over medium heat. Add the chopped onion and minced garlic. Sauté until the onion is soft.
3. Add the ground beef and cook until browned. Season with salt, black pepper, chili powder, ground cumin, and paprika.
4. In the "left drawer," place the cooked beef mixture.
5. In the "right drawer," place the diced bell peppers and canned red kidney beans.
6. Pour the crushed canned tomatoes over the beef in the "left drawer."
7. Use the "Smart Finish" icon with the "Steak" icon for the beef in the left drawer and the "Vegetables" icon for the bell peppers and beans in the right drawer.
8. Press "Start" to begin cooking. Cook it for 15 more minutes if needed
9. Once done, serve the Beef and Bean Chili.

# Beef and Pepper Stir-Fry with Rice

*Cooking Period: 30 mins /Serving Portions: 4*
*Per Serving: Calories 400, Carbs 35g, Fat 15g, Protein 30g*

## Ingredients:

- Beef sirloin or flank steak - 400g, thinly sliced
- Bell peppers - 2, sliced
- Onion - 1, sliced
- Garlic - 3 cloves, minced
- Soy sauce - 60ml
- Ginger - 10g, grated
- Cooked rice - 2 cups
- Olive oil - 30ml
- Salt - to taste
- Black pepper - to taste

## Instructions:

1. Preheat your Tower Dual Basket Air Fryer using the "Pre-Heat" icon at 180°C and wait for 3 minutes.
2. In the "left drawer," place the thinly sliced beef.
3. In a skillet, heat the olive oil over medium heat. Add the sliced onion, minced garlic, and grated ginger. Sauté until the onion is soft.
4. Add the sliced bell peppers and continue to stir-fry for a few minutes.
5. Add the soy sauce and season with salt and black pepper.
6. In the "right drawer," place the rice and water in a cake pan.
7. Use the "Smart Finish" icon with the "Steak" icon for the beef in the left drawer and the "Vegetables" icon for the stir-fried peppers and onions in the right drawer.
8. Press "Start" to begin cooking.
9. Once done, serve the Beef and Pepper Stir-Fry with Rice. A flavourful and quick British-Asian fusion dish.

# Beef and Beetroot Salad with Horseradish Dressing

*Cooking Period: 30 mins / Serving Portions: 4*
*Per Serving: Calories 350, Carbs 20g, Fat 15g, Protein 30g*

**Ingredients:**

- Beef sirloin or fillet - 500g
- Beetroot - 4, cooked and sliced
- Mixed salad greens - 200g
- Red onion - 1, thinly sliced
- Horseradish sauce - 60ml
- Olive oil - 30ml
- Lemon juice - 30ml
- Salt - to taste
- Black pepper - to taste

**Instructions:**

1. First, Preheat your Tower Dual Basket Air Fryer using the "Pre-Heat" icon at 180°C and wait for 3 minutes.
2. In the "left drawer," place the beef steak.
3. Mix the olive oil, lemon juice, horseradish sauce, salt, and black pepper in a bowl to create the dressing.
4. Grill the beef steak in the left drawer for 10-12 minutes until it reaches your desired level.
5. In the "right drawer," place the sliced beetroot and mixed salad greens.
6. Drizzle the horseradish dressing over the salad in the right drawer.
7. Use the "Smart Finish" icon with the "Steak" icon for the beef in the left drawer and set at 180°C for 12 minutes.
8. Use the "Vegetables" icon for the beetroot and salad greens in the right drawer and set at 160°C for 10 minutes. Press "Start" to begin cooking.
9. Once done, serve the Beef and Beetroot Salad with Horseradish Dressing.

# Beef Steak with Asparagus

*Cooking Period: 12 mins / Serving Portions: 2*
*Per Serving: Calories 492, Carbs 4.4g, Fat 26.5g, Protein 56.9g*

**Ingredients:**

- Striploin steaks - 2 (170-g)
- Butter - 20g, softened
- Salt and ground black pepper - to taste
- Asparagus - ½ lb.

**Instructions:**

1. Coat each steak with butter and then, season with salt and black pepper.
2. Preheat your Tower Dual Basket Air Fryer using the "Pre-Heat" icon at 180°C and wait for 3 minutes.
3. In the "left drawer," place the steaks.
4. In the "right drawer," place the asparagus.
5. Use the "Smart Finish" icon with the "Steak" icon for the beef in the left drawer and set at 180°C for 12 minutes.
6. Use the "Vegetables" icon for the asparagus in the right drawer and set at 160°C for 10 minutes. Press "Start" to begin cooking.
7. Once done, serve the steaks with your asparagus.

# Pork and Leek Casserole

*Cooking Period: 40 mins / Serving Portions: 4*
*Per Serving: Calories 350, Carbs 20g, Fat 15g, Protein 25g*

**Ingredients:**

- Pork loin or shoulder - 500g, cubed
- Leeks - 2, sliced
- Onion - 1, chopped
- Garlic - 3 cloves, minced
- Carrots - 2, sliced
- Potatoes - 2, cubed
- Pork or vegetable broth - 500ml
- Olive oil - 30ml
- Thyme - 10g, dried
- Salt - to taste
- Black pepper - to taste

**Instructions:**

1. Preheat your Tower Dual Basket Air Fryer using the "Pre-Heat" and wait for 3 minutes.
2. In the "left drawer," place the cubed pork.
3. In a skillet, heat the olive oil over medium heat. Add the chopped onion and minced garlic. Sauté until the onion is soft.
4. Add the sliced leeks, carrots, and cubed potatoes. Stir for a few minutes.
5. Pour the pork or vegetable broth over the vegetables and season with dried thyme, salt, and black pepper.
6. Manually set the temperature at 180°C for 30 minutes.
7. Press "Start" to begin cooking.
8. Once done, serve the Pork and Leek Casserole.

# Pork Stuffed Cabbage Rolls

*Cooking Period: 20 mins / Serving Portions: 8*
*Per Serving: Calories 193, Carbs 17g, Fat 4.5g, Protein 20g*

**Ingredients:**

- Ground pork - 500g
- Cooked rice - 140g
- Egg - 1
- Onion - 1, chopped
- Garlic - 3 cloves, minced
- Paprika - 10g
- Salt - to taste
- Black pepper - to taste
- Milk - 60ml
- Cabbage leaves - 16

**Instructions:**

1. Heat a lightly greased non-skillet over medium-high heat and cook the pork for around 8-10 minutes.
2. Remove from the heat and discard any grease.
3. Transfer the cooked pork into a bowl and set aside to cool.
4. In the bowl of pork, add remaining ingredients except for cabbage leaves and blend to incorporate thoroughly.
5. Arrange the cabbage leaves onto a smooth surface.
6. Place the pork mixture on one end of each leaf and then roll up.
7. Preheat your Tower Dual Basket Air Fryer using the "Pre-Heat" icon at 180°C and wait for 3 minutes.
8. Place the cabbage rolls into both drawers, seam-sides down.
9. Use the "Match Cook" icon to set the same time and temperature for both drawers, 10 minutes at 160°C, using the "Vegetable" icon.
10. Once done, serve the Cabbage Rolls.

# Pork and Pineapple Skewers

*Cooking Period: 12 mins* / *Serving Portions: 8*
*Per Serving: Calories 388, Carbs 13.9g, Fat 23.1g, Protein 31.8g*

## Ingredients:

- Pork loin or shoulder - 900g, cubed
- Olive oil - 60ml
- 1 tablespoon jerk seasoning
- Salt - to taste
- Black pepper - to taste
- Bell peppers - 4, seeded and cubed
- Canned pineapple chunks - 560g, drained
- Paprika - 15g
- Jerk sauce - 80g
- Wooden skewers - 16, soaked in water

## Instructions:

1. In a bowl, mix together the pork cubes, jerk seasoning, salt, pepper and 30ml of oil.
2. Cover the bowl and refrigerate overnight.
3. In a large bowl, add bell pepper, salt, pepper and remaining oil and toss to combine.
4. Thread the pork, bell pepper and pineapple onto skewers.
5. Preheat your Tower Dual Basket Air Fryer using the "Pre-Heat" icon at 180°C and wait for 3 minutes.
6. Place the skewers into both drawers.
7. Use the "Match Cook" icon to set the same time and temperature for both drawers, 12 minutes at 180°C, using the "Steak" icon.
8. Once done, serve the Pork Skewers with your favorite dipping sauce.

# Pork Chops with Tomato & Onion

*Cooking Period: 680 mins* / *Serving Portions: 4*
*Per Serving: Calories 400, Carbs 3.9g, Fat 50.1g, Protein 38g*

## Ingredients:

- Olive oil - 45ml
- Garlic cloves - 2, minced
- Fresh rosemary - 5g, chopped
- Fresh parsley - 5g, chopped
- Dijon mustard - 20g
- Salt - to taste
- Black pepper - to taste
- Pork chops - 4 (150-g)
- Tomatoes - 4, cut into thick slices
- Large red onions - 1, sliced

## Instructions:

1. In a bowl, mix together the garlic, herbs, oil, mustard, coriander, sugar, and salt.
2. Add the pork chops and generously coat with marinade.
3. Cover and refrigerate for about 2-3 hours.
4. Remove chops from the refrigerator and set aside at room temperature for about 30 minutes.
5. In another bowl, add tomato, onion, remaining oil, salt and pepper and gently toss to incorporate.
6. Preheat your Tower Dual Basket Air Fryer using the "Pre-Heat" icon at 180°C and wait for 3 minutes.
7. In the "left drawer," place the pork chops.
8. In the "right drawer," place the tomato mixture.
9. Use the "Smart Finish" icon with the "Steak" icon for the pork in the left drawer and set at 180°C for 14 minutes.
10. Use the "Vegetables" icon for the tomato mixture in the right drawer and set at 160°C for 10 minutes. Press "Start" to begin cooking.
11. Once done, serve the Pork chops with tomato mixture.

# Pork with Bell Peppers

*Cooking Period: 10 mins / Serving Portions: 4*
*Per Serving: Calories 372, Carbs 11.2g, Fat 16.3g, Protein 44.6g*

**Ingredients:**

- Olive oil - 60ml
- Dried oregano - 10g, crushed
- Onion powder - 5g
- Garlic powder - 5g
- Red chili powder - 5g
- Paprika - 5g
- Salt - to taste
- Pork tenderloin - 570g, cut into strips
- Large bell peppers - 3, seeded and sliced
- Large onion - 1, sliced

**Instructions:**

1. In a large bowl, mix together the oil, oregano and spices.
2. Transfer half of oil mixture into a second bowl with pork strips and mix well.
3. I the bowl of remaining bell peppers, onion, and oil and mix until well combined.
4. First, preheat your Tower Dual Basket Air Fryer using the "Pre-Heat" icon at 180°C.
5. In the "left drawer," place the cubed pork.
6. In the "right drawer," place the bell pepper mixture.
7. Use the "Smart Finish" icon with the "Steak" icon for the pork in the left drawer and set at 180°C for 8 minutes.
8. Use the "Vegetables" icon for the bell pepper mixture in the right drawer and set at 160°C for 10 minutes. Press "Start" to begin cooking.
9. Once done, transfer the pork strips and bell pepper mixture into a large bowl and blend thoroughly.
10. Serve hot.

# BBQ Pork Chops

*Cooking Period: 14 mins / Serving Portions: 6*
*Per Serving: Calories 757, Carbs 7.6g, Fat 51g, Protein 51.1g*

**Ingredients:**

- Pork chops - 6 (226-gram)
- BBQ sauce - 115g
- Salt - to taste
- Black pepper - to taste

**Instructions:**

1. With a meat tenderizer, tenderize the chops completely.
2. Sprinkle the chops with a little salt and black pepper.
3. In a large bowl, add the BBQ and chops and mix well.
4. Refrigerate, covered for about 6-8 hours.
5. Preheat your Tower Dual Basket Air Fryer using the "Pre-Heat" icon at 180°C and wait for 3 minutes.
6. Place the chops into both drawers.
7. Use the "Match Cook" icon to set the same time and temperature for both drawers, 14 minutes at 180°C, using the "Steak" icon.
8. Press "Start" to begin cooking.
9. Once done, serve the pork chops hot.

# Air-Fried Green Beans

*Cooking Period: 20 mins / Serving Portions: 4*
*Per Serving: Calories 60, Carbs 10g, Fat 2g, Protein 2g*

**Ingredients:**

- Green beans - 400g
- Olive oil - 30ml
- Garlic - 2 cloves, minced
- Lemon zest - from 1 lemon
- Salt - to taste
- Black pepper - to taste

**Instructions:**

1. Preheat your Tower Dual Basket Air Fryer using the "Pre-Heat" icon, but adjust the temperature to 160°C.
2. In the "left drawer," place the green beans.
3. Drizzle olive oil over the green beans, and add minced garlic, lemon zest, salt, and black pepper. Toss to coat.
4. Use the "vegetable" icon to cook the green beans in the left drawer at 160°C for 10 minutes.
5. Press "Start" to begin cooking.
6. Once done, serve the Air-Fried Green Beans.

# Roasted Brussels Sprouts

*Cooking Period: 25 mins / Serving Portions: 4*
*Per Serving: Calories 70, Carbs 10g, Fat 3g, Protein 3g*

**Ingredients:**

- Brussels sprouts - 400g, halved
- Olive oil - 30ml
- Balsamic vinegar - 30ml
- Garlic - 2 cloves, minced
- Salt - to taste
- Black pepper - to taste

**Instructions:**

1. Preheat your Tower Dual Basket Air Fryer using the "Preheat" icon at 180°C and wait for 3 minutes.
2. In the "left drawer," place the halved Brussels sprouts.
3. Drizzle olive oil and balsamic vinegar over the Brussels sprouts. Add minced garlic, salt, and black pepper. Toss to coat.
4. Use the "Vegetable" icon to cook the Brussels sprouts in the left drawer at 180°C for 20 minutes.
5. Press "Start" to begin cooking.
6. Once done, serve the Roasted Brussels Sprouts.

# Crispy Carrot Chips

*Cooking Period: 20 mins* / *Serving Portions: 4*
*Per Serving: Calories 80, Carbs 15g, Fat 3g, Protein 1g*

**Ingredients:**

- Carrots - 400g, thinly sliced into chips
- Olive oil - 30ml
- Paprika - 10g
- Salt - to taste
- Black pepper - to taste

**Instructions:**

1. Preheating is crucial, so preheat your Tower Dual Basket Air Fryer before using it.
2. In the "left drawer," place the thinly sliced carrot chips.
3. Drizzle olive oil over the carrot chips and season with paprika, salt, and black pepper. Toss to coat.
4. Use the "vegetable" icon to cook the carrot chips in the left drawer at 180°C for 10 minutes.
5. Press "Start" to begin cooking.
6. Once done, serve the Crispy Carrot Chips.

# Air-Fried Asparagus

*Cooking Period: 15 mins* / *Serving Portions: 4*
*Per Serving: Calories 40, Carbs 5g, Fat 2g, Protein 3g*

**Ingredients:**

- Asparagus - 400g
- Olive oil - 30ml
- Lemon juice - 30ml
- Garlic - 2 cloves, minced
- Parmesan cheese - 20g, grated
- Salt - to taste
- Black pepper - to taste

**Instructions:**

1. Preheat your Tower Dual Basket Air Fryer using the "Pre-Heat" icon at 180°C and wait for 3 minutes.
2. In the "left drawer," place the asparagus.
3. Drizzle olive oil and lemon juice over the asparagus, and add minced garlic, grated Parmesan cheese, salt, and black pepper. Toss to coat.
4. Use the "Vegetable" icon to cook the asparagus in the left drawer at 180°C for 10 minutes.
5. Press "Start" to begin cooking.
6. Dish out nice and hot once it's done.

# Zucchini Fritters

*Cooking Period: 20 mins / Serving Portions: 4*
*Per Serving: Calories 80, Carbs 10g, Fat 4g, Protein 3g*

**Ingredients:**

- Zucchini - 400g, grated and squeezed dry
- Egg - 1
- Onion - 1, finely chopped
- Flour - 30g
- Parmesan cheese - 20g, grated
- Olive oil - 30ml
- Salt - to taste
- Black pepper - to taste

**Instructions:**

1. Firstly, preheat your Tower Dual Basket Air Fryer using the "Pre-Heat" icon.
2. Combine the grated zucchini, finely chopped onion, egg, flour, grated Parmesan cheese, salt, and black pepper in a mixing bowl. Mix well.
3. In the "left drawer," scoop spoonfuls of the zucchini mixture to form fritters.
4. Drizzle olive oil over the fritters.
5. Use the "Vegetable" icon to cook the zucchini fritters in the left drawer.
6. Press "Start" to begin cooking.
7. Once done, serve the Zucchini Fritters.

# Parmesan Roasted Cauliflower

*Cooking Period: 20 mins / Serving Portions: 4*
*Per Serving: Calories 70, Carbs 5g, Fat 4g, Protein 3g*

**Ingredients:**

- Cauliflower - 1 head
- Olive oil - 30ml
- Parmesan cheese - 30g, grated
- Garlic - 2 cloves, minced
- Thyme - 10g, dried
- Salt - to taste
- Black pepper - to taste

**Instructions:**

1. Preheat your Tower Dual Basket Air Fryer using the "Pre-Heat" icon at 180°C and wait for 3 minutes.
2. In the "left drawer," place the cauliflower.
3. Drizzle olive oil over the cauliflower, and add minced garlic, grated Parmesan cheese, dried thyme, salt, and black pepper. Toss to coat.
4. Use the "Vegetable" icon to roast the cauliflower in the left drawer at 180°C for 10 minutes.
5. Press "Start" to begin cooking.
6. Once done, serve the Parmesan Roasted Cauliflower. A flavourful and healthy dish for your loved ones.

# Butternut Squash Fries

*Cooking Period: 20 mins / Serving Portions: 4*
*Per Serving: Calories 90, Carbs 15g, Fat 3g, Protein 1g*

**Ingredients:**

- Butternut squash - 400g, cut into fries
- Olive oil - 30ml
- Paprika - 10g
- Salt - to taste
- Black pepper - to taste

**Instructions:**

1. To start cooking, let's preheat your Tower Dual Basket Air Fryer using the "Pre-Heat" icon.
2. In the "left drawer," place the butternut squash fries.
3. Drizzle olive oil over the fries and season with paprika, salt, and black pepper. Toss to coat.
4. Use the "Vegetable" icon to cook the butternut squash fries in the left drawer at 180°C for 10 minutes.
5. Press "Start" to begin cooking.
6. Once done, serve the Butternut Squash Fries.

# Garlic Roasted Mushrooms

*Cooking Period: 20 mins / Serving Portions: 4*
*Per Serving: Calories 60, Carbs 5g, Fat 4g, Protein 2g*

**Ingredients:**

- Button mushrooms - 400g
- Olive oil - 30ml
- Garlic - 3 cloves, minced
- Thyme - 10g, dried
- Salt - to taste
- Black pepper - to taste

**Instructions:**

1. Preheat your Tower Dual Basket Air Fryer using the "Pre-Heat" icon at 180°C and wait for 3 minutes.
2. In the "left drawer," place the button mushrooms.
3. Drizzle olive oil over the mushrooms, and add minced garlic, dried thyme, salt, and black pepper. Toss to coat.
4. Use the "Vegetable" icon to roast the mushrooms in the left drawer at 180°C; adjust the time to 15 minutes.
5. Press "Start" to begin cooking.
6. Once done, serve the Garlic Roasted Mushrooms. A flavourful and aromatic side dish.

# Sweet Potato Wedges

*Cooking Period: 20 mins /Serving Portions: 4*
*Per Serving: Calories 80, Carbs 15g, Fat 2g, Protein 2g*

**Ingredients:**

- Sweet potatoes - 400g, cut into wedges
- Olive oil - 30ml
- Paprika - 10g
- Salt - to taste
- Black pepper - to taste

**Instructions:**

1. Preheat your Tower Dual Basket Air Fryer using the "Pre-Heat" icon at 180°C and wait for 3 minutes.
2. In the "left drawer," place the sweet potato wedges.
3. Drizzle olive oil over the wedges and season with paprika, salt, and black pepper. Toss to coat.
4. Use the "Vegetable" icon to cook the sweet potato wedges in the left drawer for 15 minutes.
5. Press "Start" to begin cooking.
6. Once done, serve the Sweet Potato Wedges. It is a delightful and healthier vegetable dish.

# Curried Eggplant Slices

*Cooking Period: 20 mins /Serving Portions: 4*
*Per Serving: Calories 70, Carbs 10g, Fat 3g, Protein 2g*

**Ingredients:**

- Eggplant - 1, sliced into rounds
- Olive oil - 30ml
- Curry powder - 10g
- Salt - to taste
- Black pepper - to taste

**Instructions:**

1. Start by preheating your Tower Dual Basket Air Fryer using the "Pre-Heat" icon at 180°C and wait for 3 minutes.
2. In the "left drawer," place the eggplant slices.
3. Drizzle olive oil over the eggplant and season with curry powder, salt, and black pepper. Toss to coat.
4. Use the "Vegetable" icon to cook the eggplant slices in the left drawer at 180°C for 10 minutes.
5. Press "Start" to begin cooking.
6. Once done, serve the Curried Eggplant Slices. A flavourful and exotic vegetable dish.

# Desserts

# Apple Crisp

*Cooking Period: 20 mins / Serving Portions: 4*
*Per Serving: Calories 150, Carbs 30g, Fat 3g, Protein 2g*

**Ingredients:**

- Apples - 4, sliced
- Cinnamon - 10g
- Oats - 30g

**Instructions:**

1. Preheat your Tower Dual Basket Air Fryer using the "Pre-Heat" icon at 180°C and wait for 3 minutes.
2. In the "left drawer," place the sliced apples.
3. Toss the apple slices with cinnamon and oats.
4. Use the "Cake" icon to air fry the apples in the left drawer at 180°C for 15 minutes.
5. Press "Start" to begin cooking.
6. Once done, serve the Apple Crisp.

# Baked Bananas

*Cooking Period: 15 mins / Serving Portions: 4*
*Per Serving: Calories 120, Carbs 30g, Fat 1g, Protein 1g*

**Ingredients:**

- Bananas - 4, sliced lengthwise
- Cinnamon - 10g
- Honey - 30ml

**Instructions:**

1. Preheat your Tower Dual Basket Air Fryer using the "Pre-Heat" icon at 180°C and wait for 3 minutes.
2. In the "left drawer," place the sliced bananas.
3. Sprinkle the bananas with cinnamon and drizzle honey over them.
4. Use the "Vegetable" icon to air fry the bananas in the left drawer at 180°C for 10 minutes.
5. Press "Start" to begin cooking.
6. Once done, serve the Baked Bananas.

# Air-Fried Scones

*Cooking Period: 15 mins /Serving Portions: 4*
*Per Serving: Calories 200, Carbs 30g, Fat 8g, Protein 4g*

**Ingredients:**

- Scone dough - Prepared
- Flour - for dusting
- Clotted cream and jam - for serving (optional)

**Instructions:**

1. Preheat your Tower Dual Basket Air Fryer using the "Pre-Heat" icon; it is an extremely important part.
2. In the "left drawer," place small rounds of scone dough.
3. Use the "Cake" icon to air fry the scones in the left drawer at 160°C for 20 minutes.
4. Press "Start" to begin cooking.
5. Once done, serve the Air-Fried Scones. Enjoy these traditional treats, and serve with clotted cream and jam if desired.

# Oatmeal Cookies

*Cooking Period: 12 mins /Serving Portions: 4*
*Per Serving: Calories 160, Carbs 25g, Fat 7g, Protein 2g*

**Ingredients:**

- All-purpose flour - 120g
- Rolled oats - 90g
- Unsalted butter, softened - 115g
- Brown sugar - 100g
- Granulated sugar - 50g
- Egg - 1
- Vanilla extract - 2.5 ml
- Baking soda - 2.3g
- Salt - to taste
- Raisins (optional) - 60g
- Chopped nuts (optional) - 60g

**Instructions:**

1. Combine the all-purpose flour, rolled oats, baking soda, and salt in a medium-sized bowl. Mix well and set aside.
2. In another bowl, cream the softened unsalted butter, brown sugar, and granulated sugar until the mixture is light and fluffy. This can be done using an electric mixer or by hand.
3. Beat the egg and vanilla extract until the mixture is smooth and well combined.
4. Gradually add the dry ingredient mixture to the wet ingredients, mixing until just incorporated. If desired, fold in raisins and chopped nuts.
5. Preheat your Tower Dual Basket Air Fryer using the "Pre-Heat" icon at 160°C and wait for 3 minutes.
6. Dust your work surface with a bit of flour. Shape small portions of the oatmeal cookie dough into round cookies.
7. Place the oatmeal cookies in the "left drawer" of the air fryer, leaving some space between them.
8. Use the "Vegetable" icon to air fry the cookies in the left drawer at 160°C for 10 minutes.
9. Press "Start" to begin cooking.
10. Once done, serve the Oatmeal Cookies.

# Fruit Skewers

*Cooking Period: 15 mins / Serving Portions: 4*
*Per Serving: Calories 80, Carbs 20g, Fat 0g, Protein 1g*

**Ingredients:**

- Pineapple chunks - 200g
- Strawberries - 200g
- Kiwi - 2, peeled and sliced
- Wooden skewers - soaked in water
- Honey - 30ml (for drizzling, optional)

**Instructions:**

1. Preheat your Tower Dual Basket Air Fryer using the "Pre-Heat" icon at 160°C and wait for 3 minutes.
2. Thread chunks of pineapple, strawberries, and kiwi onto the wooden skewers.
3. In the "left drawer," place the fruit skewers.
4. Use the "Vegetable" icon to air fry the fruit skewers in the left drawer at 160°C for 10 minutes.
5. Press "Start" to begin cooking.
6. Once done, drizzle with honey if desired and serve the Fruit Skewers.

# Baked Plums

*Cooking Period: 12 mins / Serving Portions: 4*
*Per Serving: Calories 60, Carbs 15g, Fat 0g, Protein 1g*

**Ingredients:**

- Plums - 4, halved and pitted
- Sugar - 20g

**Instructions:**

1. Preheat your Tower Dual Basket Air Fryer using the "Pre-Heat" icon at 160°C and wait for 3 minutes.
2. In the "left drawer," place the halved and pitted plums.
3. Sprinkle the plums with sugar.
4. Use the "Vegetable" icon to air fry the plums in the left drawer at 160°C for 10 minutes.
5. Press "Start" to begin cooking.
6. Once done, serve the Baked Plums. Enjoy these soft and juicy plums.

# Air-Fried Rice Pudding

Cooking Period: 20 mins | Serving Portions: 4
Per Serving: Calories 180, Carbs 40g, Fat 1g, Protein 3g

**Ingredients:**

- Cooked rice - 400g
- Milk - 480ml
- Sugar - 100g
- Vanilla extract - 5ml

**Instructions:**

1. Combine the cooked rice, milk, sugar, and vanilla extract in a mixing bowl. Mix well.
2. Preheat your Tower Dual Basket Air Fryer using the "Pre-Heat" icon at 160°C and wait for 3 minutes.
3. In the "left drawer," place the rice pudding mixture.
4. Use the "Cake" icon to air fry the rice pudding in the left drawer at 160°C for 25 minutes.
5. Press "Start" to begin cooking.
6. Once done, serve the Air-Fried Rice Pudding.

# Poached Pears in Red Wine

Cooking Period: 25 mins | Serving Portions: 4
Per Serving: Calories 150, Carbs 40g, Fat 0g, Protein 1g

**Ingredients:**

- Pears - 4, peeled and cored
- Red wine - 750ml
- Sugar - 200g
- Cinnamon sticks - 2
- Star anise - 2
- Orange peel - from 1 orange
- Cloves - 6
- Vanilla pod - 1, split lengthwise

**Instructions:**

1. Combine the red wine, sugar, cinnamon sticks, star anise, orange peel, cloves, and split vanilla pod in a deep pan. Bring this mixture to a simmer.
2. Carefully add the peeled and cored pears to the red wine mixture. Make sure they are fully submerged in the liquid.
3. Poach the pears in the red wine mixture for about 20 minutes or until tender but still holding their shape.
4. While the pears are poaching, preheat your Tower Dual Basket Air Fryer using the "Preheat" icon at 180°C and wait for 3 minutes.
5. In the "left drawer," place the peeled and cored poached pears.
6. Use the "Vegetable" icon to air fry the pears in the left drawer at 180°C for 10 minutes.
7. Press "Start" to begin cooking.
8. Once done, serve the Poached Pears in Red Wine. This elegant dessert is a lovely combination of fruity, spicy, and aromatic flavors.

# Brownie Muffins

Cooking Period: 22 mins | Serving Portions: 12
Per Serving: Calories 241, Carbs 36.9g, Fat 9.8g, Protein 2.6g

**Ingredients:**

- Non-stick baking spray
- Betty Crocker fudge brownie mix - 1 package
- Egg - 1
- Water - 10ml
- Walnuts - 25g, chopped
- Vegetable oil - 90ml

**Instructions:**

1. Grease 12 muffin molds with baking spray.
2. In a bowl, add all the ingredients and mix well.
3. Place mixture into the prepared muffin molds.
4. Preheat your Tower Dual Basket Air Fryer using the "Pre-Heat" icon at 180°C and wait for 3 minutes.
5. Place the muffin molds into both drawers.
6. Use the "Match Cook" function to set the same time and temperature for both drawers, 22 minutes at 160°C, using the "Cake" icon.
7. Press "Start" to begin cooking.
8. Once done, remove the muffin molds from Air Fryer and place onto a wire rack to cool for about 10 minutes.
9. Carefully invert the muffins onto wire rack to completely cool before serving.

# Berry Crumble

Cooking Period: 20 mins | Serving Portions: 4
Per Serving: Calories 200, Carbs 40g, Fat 5g, Protein 3g

**Ingredients:**

- Mixed fresh berries - 400g
- Oats - 60g
- Flour - 60g
- Butter - 60g
- Sugar - 60g

**Instructions:**

1. Combine the oats, flour, sugar, and butter in a mixing bowl. Use your fingers to rub the ingredients together until they resemble breadcrumbs.
2. Preheat your Tower Dual Basket Air Fryer using the "Preheat" icon at 160°C and wait for 3 minutes.
3. In the "left drawer," place the mixed fresh berries.
4. Sprinkle the crumble topping over the berries.
5. Use the "Cake" icon to air fry the berry crumble in the left drawer at 160°C, and adjust the time for 18 minutes.
6. Press "Start" to begin cooking.
7. Once done, serve the Berry Crumble. Enjoy this crisp and fruity dessert.

# Conclusion

Your journey with the Tower Dual Basket Air Fryer is just starting, and it's an exciting one. You've got to know this fantastic kitchen buddy, its amazing perks, and how easy it is to use. You've also learned how to keep it in tip-top shape. It's time for the fun part - trying out scrumptious recipes.

We want you to enter your kitchen with a big smile and a sense of adventure. Don't worry if a dish doesn't turn out perfect - that's how we learn. Cooking is like an art, and it's supposed to be fun and creative. So, don't be afraid to experiment, try new things, and put your twist on recipes.

Cooking should bring you joy and make you proud of what you create. It's about sharing tasty meals with friends and family. As you explore the recipes in this book, enjoy yourself, be patient, and never stop exploring. We wish you the best of luck on your cooking journey. May your kitchen be filled with delicious smells and your table with happy faces.

Printed in Great Britain
by Amazon

41469567R00044